THE COMPLETE WORKS OF
HENRY WADSWORTH LONGFELLOW

THE COMPLETE WORKS OF
HENRY WADSWORTH LONGFELLOW

Volume IV

BIBLIOBAZAAR

THE COMPLETE WORKS OF
HENRY WADSWORTH LONGFELLOW

CONTENTS

JUDAS MACCABAEUS.

ACT I.

The Citadel of Antiochus at Jerusalem.

SCENE I.—ANTIOCHUS; JASON.

ANTIOCHUS.

 O Antioch, my Antioch, my city!
 Queen of the East! my solace, my delight!
 The dowry of my sister Cleopatra
 When she was wed to Ptolemy, and now
 Won back and made more wonderful by me!
 I love thee, and I long to be once more
 Among the players and the dancing women
 Within thy gates, and bathe in the Orontes,
 Thy river and mine. O Jason, my High-Priest,
 For I have made thee so, and thou art mine,
 Hast thou seen Antioch the Beautiful?

JASON.

 Never, my Lord.

ANTIOCHUS.

 Then hast thou never seen
 The wonder of the world. This city of David
 Compared with Antioch is but a village,
 And its inhabitants compared with Greeks
 Are mannerless boors.

JASON.
> They are barbarians,
> And mannerless.

ANTIOCHUS.
> They must be civilized.
> They must be made to have more gods than one;
> And goddesses besides.

JASON.
> They shall have more.

ANTIOCHUS.
> They must have hippodromes, and games, and baths,
> Stage-plays and festivals, and most of all
> The Dionysia.

JASON.
> They shall have them all.

ANTIOCHUS.
> By Heracles! but I should like to see
> These Hebrews crowned with ivy, and arrayed
> In skins of fawns, with drums and flutes and thyrsi,
> Revel and riot through the solemn streets
> Of their old town. Ha, ha! It makes me merry
> Only to think of it!—Thou dost not laugh.

JASON.
> Yea, I laugh inwardly.

ANTIOCHUS.
> The new Greek leaven
> Works slowly in this Israelitish dough!
> Have I not sacked the Temple, and on the altar
> Set up the statue of Olympian Zeus
> To Hellenize it?

JASON.

    Thou hast done all this.

ANTIOCHUS.

    As thou wast Joshua once and now art Jason,
    And from a Hebrew hast become a Greek,
    So shall this Hebrew nation be translated,
    Their very natures and their names be changed,
    And all be Hellenized.

JASON.

    It shall be done.

ANTIOCHUS.

    Their manners and their laws and way of living
    Shall all be Greek. They shall unlearn their language,
    And learn the lovely speech of Antioch.
    Where hast thou been to-day? Thou comest late.

JASON.

    Playing at discus with the other priests
    In the Gymnasium.

ANTIOCHUS.

    Thou hast done well.
    There's nothing better for you lazy priests
    Than discus-playing with the common people.
    Now tell me, Jason, what these Hebrews call me
    When they converse together at their games.

JASON.

    Antiochus Epiphanes, my Lord;
    Antiochus the Illustrious.

ANTIOCHUS.

    O, not that;
    That is the public cry; I mean the name
    They give me when they talk among themselves,
    And think that no one listens; what is that?

JASON.

> Antiochus Epimanes, my Lord!

ANTIOCHUS.

> Antiochus the Mad! Ay, that is it.
> And who hath said it? Who hath set in motion
> That sorry jest?

JASON.

> The Seven Sons insane
> Of a weird woman, like themselves insane.

ANTIOCHUS.

> I like their courage, but it shall not save them.
> They shall be made to eat the flesh of swine,
> Or they shall die. Where are they?

JASON.

> In the dungeons
> Beneath this tower.

ANTIOCHUS.

> There let them stay and starve,
> Till I am ready to make Greeks of them,
> After my fashion.

JASON.

> They shall stay and starve.—
> My Lord, the Ambassadors of Samaria
> Await thy pleasure.

ANTIOCHUS.

> Why not my displeasure?
> Ambassadors are tedious. They are men
> Who work for their own ends, and not for mine
> There is no furtherance in them. Let them go
> To Apollonius, my governor
> There in Samaria, and not trouble me.
> What do they want?

JASON.

> Only the royal sanction
> To give a name unto a nameless temple
> Upon Mount Gerizim.

ANTIOCHUS.

> Then bid them enter.
> This pleases me, and furthers my designs.
> The occasion is auspicious. Bid them enter.

SCENE II.—ANTIOCHUS; JASON; THE SAMARITAN AMBASSADORS.

ANTIOCHUS.

> Approach. Come forward; stand not at the door
> Wagging your long beards, but demean yourselves
> As doth become Ambassadors. What seek ye?

AN AMBASSADOR.

> An audience from the King.

ANTIOCHUS.

> Speak, and be brief.
> Waste not the time in useless rhetoric.
> Words are not things.

AMBASSADOR (reading). "To King Antiochus,

> The God, Epiphanes; a Memorial
> From the Sidonians, who live at Sichem."

ANTIOCHUS.

> Sidonians?

AMBASSADOR.

> Ay, my Lord.

ANTIOCHUS.

> Go on, go on!
> And do not tire thyself and me with bowing!

AMBASSADOR (reading).

"We are a colony of Medes and Persians."

ANTIOCHUS.

No, ye are Jews from one of the Ten Tribes;
Whether Sidonians or Samaritans
Or Jews of Jewry, matters not to me;
Ye are all Israelites, ye are all Jews.
When the Jews prosper, ye claim kindred with them;
When the Jews suffer, ye are Medes and Persians:
I know that in the days of Alexander
Ye claimed exemption from the annual tribute
In the Sabbatic Year, because, ye said,
Your fields had not been planted in that year.

AMBASSADOR (reading).

"Our fathers, upon certain frequent plagues,
And following an ancient superstition,
Were long accustomed to observe that day
Which by the Israelites is called the Sabbath,
And in a temple on Mount Gerizim
Without a name, they offered sacrifice.
Now we, who are Sidonians, beseech thee,
Who art our benefactor and our savior,
Not to confound us with these wicked Jews,
But to give royal order and injunction
To Apollonius in Samaria.
Thy governor, and likewise to Nicanor,
Thy procurator, no more to molest us;
And let our nameless temple now be named
The Temple of Jupiter Hellenius."

ANTIOCHUS.

This shall be done. Full well it pleaseth me
Ye are not Jews, or are no longer Jews,
But Greeks; if not by birth, yet Greeks by custom.
Your nameless temple shall receive the name
Of Jupiter Hellenius. Ye may go!

SCENE III.—ANTIOCHUS; JASON.

ANTIOCHUS.

> My task is easier than I dreamed. These people
> Meet me half-way. Jason, didst thou take note
> How these Samaritans of Sichem said
> They were not Jews? that they were Medes and Persians,
> They were Sidonians, anything but Jews?
> 'T is of good augury. The rest will follow
> Till the whole land is Hellenized.

JASON.

> My Lord,
> These are Samaritans. The tribe of Judah
> Is of a different temper, and the task
> Will be more difficult.

ANTIOCHUS.

> Dost thou gainsay me?

JASON.

> I know the stubborn nature of the Jew.
> Yesterday, Eleazer, an old man,
> Being fourscore years and ten, chose rather death
> By torture than to eat the flesh of swine.

ANTIOCHUS.

> The life is in the blood, and the whole nation
> Shall bleed to death, or it shall change its faith!

JASON.

> Hundreds have fled already to the mountains
> Of Ephraim, where Judas Maccabaeus
> Hath raised the standard of revolt against thee.

ANTIOCHUS.

> I will burn down their city, and will make it
> Waste as a wilderness. Its thoroughfares
> Shall be but furrows in a field of ashes.

It shall be sown with salt as Sodom is!
This hundred and fifty-third Olympiad
Shall have a broad and blood-red sea upon it,
Stamped with the awful letters of my name,
Antiochus the God, Epiphanes!—
Where are those Seven Sons?

JASON.

My Lord, they wait
Thy royal pleasure.

ANTIOCHUS.

They shall wait no longer!

ACT II.
The Dungeons in the Citadel.

SCENE I.—THE MOTHER of the SEVEN SONS alone,
listening.

THE MOTHER.

Be strong, my heart!
Break not till they are dead,
All, all my Seven Sons; then burst asunder,
And let this tortured and tormented soul
Leap and rush out like water through the shards
Of earthen vessels broken at a well.
O my dear children, mine in life and death,
I know not how ye came into my womb;
I neither gave you breath, nor gave you life,
And neither was it I that formed the members
Of every one of you. But the Creator,
Who made the world, and made the heavens above us,
Who formed the generation of mankind,
And found out the beginning of all things,
He gave you breath and life, and will again
Of his own mercy, as ye now regard
Not your own selves, but his eternal law.
I do not murmur, nay, I thank thee, God,

That I and mine have not been deemed unworthy
To suffer for thy sake, and for thy law,
And for the many sins of Israel.
Hark! I can hear within the sound of scourges!
I feel them more than ye do, O my sons!
But cannot come to you. I, who was wont
To wake at night at the least cry ye made,
To whom ye ran at every slightest hurt,
I cannot take you now into my lap
And soothe your pain, but God will take you all
Into his pitying arms, and comfort you,
And give you rest.

A VOICE (within).
     What wouldst thou ask of us?
     Ready are we to die, but we will never
     Transgress the law and customs of our fathers.

THE MOTHER.
     It is the Voice of my first-born! O brave
     And noble boy! Thou hast the privilege
     Of dying first, as thou wast born the first.

THE SAME VOICE (within).
     God looketh on us, and hath comfort in us;
     As Moses in his song of old declared,
     He in his servants shall be comforted.

THE MOTHER.
     I knew thou wouldst not fail!—He speaks no more,
     He is beyond all pain!

ANTIOCHUS. (within).
     If thou eat not
     Thou shalt be tortured throughout all the members
     Of thy whole body. Wilt thou eat then?

SECOND VOICE. (within).
     No.

THE MOTHER.

    It is Adaiah's voice. I tremble for him.
    I know his nature, devious as the wind,
    And swift to change, gentle and yielding always.
    Be steadfast, O my son!

THE SAME VOICE (within).

    Thou, like a fury,
    Takest us from this present life, but God,
    Who rules the world, shall raise us up again
    Into life everlasting.

THE MOTHER.

    God, I thank thee
    That thou hast breathed into that timid heart
    Courage to die for thee. O my Adaiah,
    Witness of God! if thou for whom I feared
    Canst thus encounter death, I need not fear;
    The others will not shrink.

THIRD VOICE (within).

    Behold these hands
    Held out to thee, O King Antiochus,
    Not to implore thy mercy, but to show
    That I despise them. He who gave them to me
    Will give them back again.

THE MOTHER.

    O Avilan,
    It is thy voice. For the last time I hear it;
    For the last time on earth, but not the last.
    To death it bids defiance and to torture.
    It sounds to me as from another world,
    And makes the petty miseries of this
    Seem unto me as naught, and less than naught.
    Farewell, my Avilan; nay, I should say
    Welcome, my Avilan; for I am dead

Before thee. I am waiting for the others.
Why do they linger?

FOURTH VOICE (within).
It is good, O King,
Being put to death by men, to look for hope
From God, to be raised up again by him.
But thou—no resurrection shalt thou have
To life hereafter.

THE MOTHER.
Four! already four!
Three are still living; nay, they all are living,
Half here, half there. Make haste, Antiochus,
To reunite us; for the sword that cleaves
These miserable bodies makes a door
Through which our souls, impatient of release,
Rush to each other's arms.

FIFTH VOICE (within).
Thou hast the power;
Thou doest what thou wilt. Abide awhile,
And thou shalt see the power of God, and how
He will torment thee and thy seed.

THE MOTHER.
O hasten;
Why dost thou pause? Thou who hast slain already
So many Hebrew women, and hast hung
Their murdered infants round their necks, slay me,
For I too am a woman, and these boys
Are mine. Make haste to slay us all,
And hang my lifeless babes about my neck.

SIXTH VOICE (within).
Think not,
Antiochus, that takest in hand
To strive against the God of Israel,

Thou shalt escape unpunished, for his wrath
Shall overtake thee and thy bloody house.

THE MOTHER.

One more, my Sirion, and then all is ended.
Having put all to bed, then in my turn
I will lie down and sleep as sound as they.
My Sirion, my youngest, best beloved!
And those bright golden locks, that I so oft
Have curled about these fingers, even now
Are foul with blood and dust, like a lamb's fleece,
Slain in the shambles.—Not a sound I hear.
This silence is more terrible to me
Than any sound, than any cry of pain,
That might escape the lips of one who dies.
Doth his heart fail him? Doth he fall away
In the last hour from God? O Sirion, Sirion,
Art thou afraid? I do not hear thy voice.
Die as thy brothers died. Thou must not live!

SCENE II.—THE MOTHER; ANTIOCHUS; SIRION,

THE MOTHER.

Are they all dead?

ANTIOCHUS.

Of all thy Seven Sons
One only lives. Behold them where they lie
How dost thou like this picture?

THE MOTHER.

God in heaven!
Can a man do such deeds, and yet not die
By the recoil of his own wickedness?
Ye murdered, bleeding, mutilated bodies
That were my children once, and still are mine,
I cannot watch o'er you as Rispah watched
In sackcloth o'er the seven sons of Saul,
Till water drop upon you out of heaven

And wash this blood away! I cannot mourn
As she, the daughter of Aiah, mourned the dead,
From the beginning of the barley-harvest
Until the autumn rains, and suffered not
The birds of air to rest on them by day,
Nor the wild beasts by night. For ye have died
A better death, a death so full of life
That I ought rather to rejoice than mourn.—
Wherefore art thou not dead, O Sirion?
Wherefore art thou the only living thing
Among thy brothers dead? Art thou afraid?

ANTIOCHUS.

O woman, I have spared him for thy sake,
For he is fair to look upon and comely;
And I have sworn to him by all the gods
That I would crown his life with joy and honor,
Heap treasures on him, luxuries, delights,
Make him my friend and keeper of my secrets,
If he would turn from your Mosaic Law
And be as we are; but he will not listen.

THE MOTHER.

My noble Sirion!

ANTIOCHUS.

Therefore I beseech thee,
Who art his mother, thou wouldst speak with him,
And wouldst persuade him. I am sick of blood.

THE MOTHER.

Yea, I will speak with him and will persuade him.
O Sirion, my son! have pity on me,
On me that bare thee, and that gave thee suck,
And fed and nourished thee, and brought thee up
With the dear trouble of a mother's care
Unto this age. Look on the heavens above thee,
And on the earth and all that is therein;
Consider that God made them out of things

That were not; and that likewise in this manner
Mankind was made. Then fear not this tormentor
But, being worthy of thy brethren, take
Thy death as they did, that I may receive thee
Again in mercy with them.

ANTIOCHUS.

I am mocked,
Yea, I am laughed to scorn.

SIRION.

Whom wait ye for?
Never will I obey the King's commandment,
But the commandment of the ancient Law,
That was by Moses given unto our fathers.
And thou, O godless man, that of all others
Art the most wicked, be not lifted up,
Nor puffed up with uncertain hopes, uplifting
Thy hand against the servants of the Lord,
For thou hast not escaped the righteous judgment
Of the Almighty God, who seeth all things!

ANTIOCHUS.

He is no God of mine; I fear him not.

SIRION.

My brothers, who have suffered a brief pain,
Are dead; but thou, Antiochus, shalt suffer
The punishment of pride. I offer up
My body and my life, beseeching God
That he would speedily be merciful
Unto our nation, and that thou by plagues
Mysterious and by torments mayest confess
That he alone is God.

ANTIOCHUS.

Ye both shall perish
By torments worse than any that your God,
Here or hereafter, hath in store for me.

THE MOTHER.

    My Sirion, I am proud of thee!

ANTIOCHUS.

    Be silent!
    Go to thy bed of torture in yon chamber,
    Where lie so many sleepers, heartless mother!
    Thy footsteps will not wake them, nor thy voice,
    Nor wilt thou hear, amid thy troubled dreams,
    Thy children crying for thee in the night!

THE MOTHER.

    O Death, that stretchest thy white hands to me,
    I fear them not, but press them to my lips,
    That are as white as thine; for I am Death,
    Nay, am the Mother of Death, seeing these sons
    All lying lifeless.—Kiss me, Sirion.

ACT III.
The Battle-field of Beth-horon.

SCENE I.—JUDAS MACCABAEUS in armor before his tent.

JUDAS.

    The trumpets sound; the echoes of the mountains
    Answer them, as the Sabbath morning breaks
    Over Beth-horon and its battle-field,
    Where the great captain of the hosts of God,
    A slave brought up in the brick-fields of Egypt,
    O'ercame the Amorites. There was no day
    Like that, before or after it, nor shall be.
    The sun stood still; the hammers of the hail
    Beat on their harness; and the captains set
    Their weary feet upon the necks of kings,
    As I will upon thine, Antiochus,
    Thou man of blood!—Behold the rising sun
    Strikes on the golden letters of my banner,
    Be Elohim Yehovah! Who is like
    To thee, O Lord, among the gods!—Alas!
    I am not Joshua, I cannot say,

"Sun, stand thou still on Gibeon, and thou Moon,
In Ajalon!" Nor am I one who wastes
The fateful time in useless lamentation;
But one who bears his life upon his hand
To lose it or to save it, as may best
Serve the designs of Him who giveth life.

SCENE II—JUDAS MACCABAEUS; JEWISH FUGITIVES.

JUDAS.

Who and what are ye, that with furtive steps
Steal in among our tents?

FUGITIVES.

O Maccabaeus,
Outcasts are we, and fugitives as thou art,
Jews of Jerusalem, that have escaped
From the polluted city, and from death.

JUDAS.

None can escape from death. Say that ye come
To die for Israel, and ye are welcome.
What tidings bring ye?

FUGITIVES.

Tidings of despair.
The Temple is laid waste; the precious vessels,
Censers of gold, vials and veils and crowns,
And golden ornaments, and hidden treasures,
Have all been taken from it, and the Gentiles
With revelling and with riot fill its courts,
And dally with harlots in the holy places.

JUDAS.

All this I knew before.

FUGITIVES.

Upon the altar
Are things profane, things by the law forbidden;

Nor can we keep our Sabbaths or our Feasts,
But on the festivals of Dionysus
Must walk in their processions, bearing ivy
To crown a drunken god.

JUDAS.

This too I know.
But tell me of the Jews. How fare the Jews?

FUGITIVES.

The coming of this mischief hath been sore
And grievous to the people. All the land
Is full of lamentation and of mourning.
The Princes and the Elders weep and wail;
The young men and the maidens are made feeble;
The beauty of the women hath been changed.

JUDAS.

And are there none to die for Israel?
'T is not enough to mourn. Breastplate and harness
Are better things than sackcloth. Let the women
Lament for Israel; the men should die.

FUGITIVES.

Both men and women die; old men and young:
Old Eleazer died: and Mahala
With all her Seven Sons.

JUDAS.

Antiochus,
At every step thou takest there is left
A bloody footprint in the street, by which
The avenging wrath of God will track thee out!
It is enough. Go to the sutler's tents;
Those of you who are men, put on such armor
As ye may find; those of you who are women,
Buckle that armor on; and for a watchword
Whisper, or cry aloud, "The Help of God."

SCENE III.—JUDAS MACCABAEUS; NICANOR.

NICANOR.

Hail, Judas Maccabaeus!

JUDAS.

Hail!—Who art thou
That comest here in this mysterious guise
Into our camp unheralded?

NICANOR.

A herald
Sent from Nicanor.

JUDAS.

Heralds come not thus.
Armed with thy shirt of mail from head to heel,
Thou glidest like a serpent silently
Into my presence. Wherefore dost thou turn
Thy face from me? A herald speaks his errand
With forehead unabashed. Thou art a spy sent by Nicanor.

NICANOR.

No disguise avails!
Behold my face; I am Nicanor's self.

JUDAS.

Thou art indeed Nicanor. I salute thee.
What brings thee hither to this hostile camp
Thus unattended?

NICANOR.

Confidence in thee.
Thou hast the nobler virtues of thy race,
Without the failings that attend those virtues.
Thou canst be strong, and yet not tyrannous,
Canst righteous be and not intolerant.
Let there be peace between us.

JUDAS.

> What is peace?
> Is it to bow in silence to our victors?
> Is it to see our cities sacked and pillaged,
> Our people slain, or sold as slaves, or fleeing
> At night-time by the blaze of burning towns;
> Jerusalem laid waste; the Holy Temple
> Polluted with strange gods? Are these things peace?

NICANOR.

> These are the dire necessities that wait
> On war, whose loud and bloody enginery
> I seek to stay. Let there be peace between
> Antiochus and thee.

JUDAS.

> Antiochus?
> What is Antiochus, that he should prate
> Of peace to me, who am a fugitive?
> To-day he shall be lifted up; to-morrow
> Shall not be found, because he is returned
> Unto his dust; his thought has come to nothing.
> There is no peace between us, nor can be,
> Until this banner floats upon the walls
> Of our Jerusalem.

NICANOR.

> Between that city
> And thee there lies a waving wall of tents,
> Held by a host of forty thousand foot,
> And horsemen seven thousand. What hast thou
> To bring against all these?

JUDAS.

> The power of God,
> Whose breath shall scatter your white tents abroad,
> As flakes of snow.

NICANOR.

Your Mighty One in heaven
Will not do battle on the Seventh Day;
It is his day of rest.

JUDAS.

Silence, blasphemer.
Go to thy tents.

NICANOR.

Shall it be war or peace?

JUDAS.

War, war, and only war. Go to thy tents
That shall be scattered, as by you were scattered
The torn and trampled pages of the Law,
Blown through the windy streets.

NICANOR.

Farewell, brave foe!

JUDAS.

Ho, there, my captains! Have safe-conduct given
Unto Nicanor's herald through the camp,
And come yourselves to me.—Farewell, Nicanor!

SCENE IV.—JUDAS MACCABAEUS; CAPTAINS AND
SOLDIERS.

JUDAS.

The hour is come. Gather the host together
For battle. Lo, with trumpets and with songs
The army of Nicanor comes against us.
Go forth to meet them, praying in your hearts,
And fighting with your hands.

CAPTAINS.

Look forth and see!
The morning sun is shining on their shields

Of gold and brass; the mountains glisten with them,
And shine like lamps. And we who are so few
And poorly armed, and ready to faint with fasting,
How shall we fight against this multitude?

JUDAS.

The victory of a battle standeth not
In multitudes, but in the strength that cometh
From heaven above. The Lord forbid that I
Should do this thing, and flee away from them.
Nay, if our hour be come, then let us die;
Let us not stain our honor.

CAPTAINS.

'T is the Sabbath.
Wilt thou fight on the Sabbath, Maccabaeus?

JUDAS.

Ay; when I fight the battles of the Lord,
I fight them on his day, as on all others.
Have ye forgotten certain fugitives
That fled once to these hills, and hid themselves
In caves? How their pursuers camped against them
Upon the Seventh Day, and challenged them?
And how they answered not, nor cast a stone,
Nor stopped the places where they lay concealed,
But meekly perished with their wives and children,
Even to the number of a thousand souls?
We who are fighting for our laws and lives
Will not so perish.

CAPTAINS.

Lead us to the battle!

JUDAS.

And let our watchword be, "The Help of God!"
Last night I dreamed a dream; and in my vision
Beheld Onias, our High-Priest of old,
Who holding up his hands prayed for the Jews.

This done, in the like manner there appeared
An old man, and exceeding glorious,
With hoary hair, and of a wonderful
And excellent majesty. And Onias said:
"This is a lover of the Jews, who prayeth
Much for the people and the Holy City,—
God's prophet Jeremias." And the prophet
Held forth his right hand and gave unto me
A sword of gold; and giving it he said:
"Take thou this holy sword, a gift from God,
And with it thou shalt wound thine adversaries."

CAPTAINS.
    The Lord is with us!

JUDAS.
    Hark! I hear the trumpets
    Sound from Beth-horon; from the battle-field
    Of Joshua, where he smote the Amorites,
    Smote the Five Kings of Eglon and of Jarmuth,
    Of Hebron, Lachish, and Jerusalem,
    As we to-day will smite Nicanor's hosts
    And leave a memory of great deeds behind us.

CAPTAINS and SOLDIERS.
    The Help of God!

JUDAS.
    Be Elohim Yehovah!
    Lord, thou didst send thine Angel in the time
    Of Esekias, King of Israel,
    And in the armies of Sennacherib
    Didst slay a hundred fourscore and five thousand.
    Wherefore, O Lord of heaven, now also send
    Before us a good angel for a fear,
    And through the might of thy right arm let those
    Be stricken with terror that have come this day
    Against thy holy people to blaspheme!

ACT IV.

The outer Courts of the Temple at Jerusalem.

SCENE I.—JUDAS MACCABAEUS; CAPTAINS; JEWS.

JUDAS.

> Behold, our enemies are discomfited.
> Jerusalem is fallen; and our banners
> Float from her battlements, and o'er her gates
> Nicanor's severed head, a sign of terror,
> Blackens in wind and sun.

CAPTAINS.

> O Maccabaeus,
> The citadel of Antiochus, wherein
> The Mother with her Seven Sons was murdered,
> Is still defiant.

JUDAS.

> Wait.

CAPTAINS.

> Its hateful aspect
> Insults us with the bitter memories
> Of other days.

JUDAS.

> Wait; it shall disappear
> And vanish as a cloud. First let us cleanse
> The Sanctuary. See, it is become
> Waste like a wilderness. Its golden gates
> Wrenched from their hinges and consumed by fire;
> Shrubs growing in its courts as in a forest;
> Upon its altars hideous and strange idols;
> And strewn about its pavement at my feet
> Its Sacred Books, half burned and painted o'er
> With images of heathen gods.

JEWS.

Woe! woe!
Our beauty and our glory are laid waste!
The Gentiles have profaned our holy places!

(Lamentation and alarm of trumpets.)

JUDAS.

This sound of trumpets, and this lamentation,
The heart-cry of a people toward the heavens,
Stir me to wrath and vengeance. Go, my captains;
I hold you back no longer. Batter down
The citadel of Antiochus, while here
We sweep away his altars and his gods.

SCENE II.—JUDAS MACCABAEUS; JASON; JEWS,

JEWS.

Lurking among the ruins of the Temple,
Deep in its inner courts, we found this man,
Clad as High-Priest.

JUDAS.

I ask not who thou art.
I know thy face, writ over with deceit
As are these tattered volumes of the Law
With heathen images. A priest of God
Wast thou in other days, but thou art now
A priest of Satan. Traitor, thou art Jason.

JASON.

I am thy prisoner, Judas Maccabaeus,
And it would ill become me to conceal
My name or office.

JUDAS.

Over yonder gate
There hangs the head of one who was a Greek.
What should prevent me now, thou man of sin,

From hanging at its side the head of one
Who born a Jew hath made himself a Greek?

JASON.

Justice prevents thee.

JUDAS.

Justice? Thou art stained
With every crime against which the Decalogue
Thunders with all its thunder.

JASON.

If not Justice,
Then Mercy, her handmaiden.

JUDAS.

When hast thou
At any time, to any man or woman,
Or even to any little child, shown mercy?

JASON.

I have but done what King Antiochus
Commanded me.

JUDAS.

True, thou hast been the weapon
With which he struck; but hast been such a weapon,
So flexible, so fitted to his hand,
It tempted him to strike. So thou hast urged him
To double wickedness, thine own and his.
Where is this King? Is he in Antioch
Among his women still, and from his windows
Throwing down gold by handfuls, for the rabble
To scramble for?

JASON.

Nay, he is gone from there,
Gone with an army into the far East.

JUDAS.

>   And wherefore gone?

JASON.

>   I know not. For the space
>   Of forty days almost were horsemen seen
>   Running in air, in cloth of gold, and armed
>   With lances, like a band of soldiery;
>   It was a sign of triumph.

JUDAS.

>   Or of death.
>   Wherefore art thou not with him?

JASON.

>   I was left
>   For service in the Temple.

JUDAS.

>   To pollute it,
>   And to corrupt the Jews; for there are men
>   Whose presence is corruption; to be with them
>   Degrades us and deforms the things we do.

JASON.

>   I never made a boast, as some men do,
>   Of my superior virtue, nor denied
>   The weakness of my nature, that hath made me
>   Subservient to the will of other men.

JUDAS.

>   Upon this day, the five and twentieth day
>   Of the month Caslan, was the Temple here
>   Profaned by strangers,—by Antiochus
>   And thee, his instrument. Upon this day
>   Shall it be cleansed. Thou, who didst lend thyself
>   Unto this profanation, canst not be
>   A witness of these solemn services.
>   There can be nothing clean where thou art present.

The people put to death Callisthenes,
Who burned the Temple gates; and if they find thee
Will surely slay thee. I will spare thy life
To punish thee the longer. Thou shalt wander
Among strange nations. Thou, that hast cast out
So many from their native land, shalt perish
In a strange land. Thou, that hast left so many
Unburied, shalt have none to mourn for thee,
Nor any solemn funerals at all,
Nor sepulchre with thy fathers.—Get thee hence!

(Music. Procession of Priests and people,
with citherns, harps, and cymbals. JUDAS
MACCABAEUS puts himself at their
head, and they go into the inner courts.)

SCENE III.—JASON, alone.

JASON.

Through the Gate Beautiful I see them come
With branches and green boughs and leaves of palm,
And pass into the inner courts. Alas!
I should be with them, should be one of them,
But in an evil hour, an hour of weakness,
That cometh unto all, I fell away
From the old faith, and did not clutch the new,
Only an outward semblance of belief;
For the new faith I cannot make mine own,
Not being born to it. It hath no root
Within me. I am neither Jew nor Greek,
But stand between them both, a renegade
To each in turn; having no longer faith
In gods or men. Then what mysterious charm,
What fascination is it chains my feet,
And keeps me gazing like a curious child
Into the holy places, where the priests
Have raised their altar?—Striking stones together,
They take fire out of them, and light the lamps
In the great candlestick. They spread the veils,

And set the loaves of showbread on the table.
The incense burns; the well-remembered odor
Comes wafted unto me, and takes me back
To other days. I see myself among them
As I was then; and the old superstition
Creeps over me again!—A childish fancy!—
And hark! they sing with citherns and with cymbals,
And all the people fall upon their faces,
Praying and worshipping!—I will away
Into the East, to meet Antiochus
Upon his homeward journey, crowned with triumph.
Alas! to-day I would give everything
To see a friend's face, or to hear a voice
That had the slightest tone of comfort in it!

ACT V.
The Mountains of Ecbatana.

SCENE I.—ANTIOCHUS; PHILIP; ATTENDANTS.

ANTIOCHUS.

Here let us rest awhile. Where are we, Philip?
What place is this?

PHILIP.

Ecbatana, my Lord;
And yonder mountain range is the Orontes.

ANTIOCHUS.

The Orontes is my river at Antioch.
Why did I leave it? Why have I been tempted
By coverings of gold and shields and breastplates
To plunder Elymais, and be driven
From out its gates, as by a fiery blast
Out of a furnace?

PHILIP.

These are fortune's changes.

ANTIOCHUS.

    What a defeat it was! The Persian horsemen
    Came like a mighty wind, the wind Khamaseen,
    And melted us away, and scattered us
    As if we were dead leaves, or desert sand.

PHILIP.

    Be comforted, my Lord; for thou hast lost
    But what thou hadst not.

ANTIOCHUS.

    I, who made the Jews
    Skip like the grasshoppers, am made myself
    To skip among these stones.

PHILIP.

    Be not discouraged.
    Thy realm of Syria remains to thee;
    That is not lost nor marred.

ANTIOCHUS.

    O, where are now
    The splendors of my court, my baths and banquets?
    Where are my players and my dancing women?
    Where are my sweet musicians with their pipes,
    That made me merry in the olden time?
    I am a laughing-stock to man and brute.
    The very camels, with their ugly faces,
    Mock me and laugh at me.

PHILIP.

    Alas! my Lord,
    It is not so. If thou wouldst sleep awhile,
    All would be well.

ANTIOCHUS.

    Sleep from mine eyes is gone,
    And my heart faileth me for very care.
    Dost thou remember, Philip, the old fable

Told us when we were boys, in which the bear
Going for honey overturns the hive,
And is stung blind by bees? I am that beast,
Stung by the Persian swarms of Elymais.

PHILIP.

When thou art come again to Antioch
These thoughts will be as covered and forgotten
As are the tracks of Pharaoh's chariot-wheels
In the Egyptian sands.

ANTIOCHUS.

Ah! when I come
Again to Antioch! When will that be?
Alas! alas!

SCENE II—ANTIOCHUS; PHILIP; A MESSENGER

MESSENGER.

May the King live forever!

ANTIOCHUS.

Who art thou, and whence comest thou?

MESSENGER.

My Lord,
I am a messenger from Antioch,
Sent here by Lysias.

ANTIOCHUS.

A strange foreboding
Of something evil overshadows me.
I am no reader of the Jewish Scriptures;
I know not Hebrew; but my High-Priest Jason,
As I remember, told me of a Prophet
Who saw a little cloud rise from the sea
Like a man's hand and soon the heaven was black
With clouds and rain. Here, Philip, read; I cannot;

I see that cloud. It makes the letters dim
Before mine eyes.

PHILIP (reading).
"To King Antiochus,
The God, Epiphanes."

ANTIOCHUS.
O mockery!
Even Lysias laughs at me!—Go on, go on.

PHILIP (reading).
"We pray thee hasten thy return. The realm
Is falling from thee. Since thou hast gone from us
The victories of Judas Maccabaeus
Form all our annals. First he overthrew
Thy forces at Beth-horon, and passed on,
And took Jerusalem, the Holy City.
And then Emmaus fell; and then Bethsura;
Ephron and all the towns of Galaad,
And Maccabaeus marched to Carnion."

ANTIOCHUS.
Enough, enough! Go call my chariot-men;
We will drive forward, forward, without ceasing,
Until we come to Antioch. My captains,
My Lysias, Gorgias, Seron, and Nicanor,
Are babes in battle, and this dreadful Jew
Will rob me of my kingdom and my crown.
My elephants shall trample him to dust;
I will wipe out his nation, and will make
Jerusalem a common burying-place,
And every home within its walls a tomb!

(Throws up his hands, and sinks into the
arms of attendants, who lay him upon
a bank.)

PHILIP.

>Antiochus! Antiochus! Alas,
>The King is ill! What is it, O my Lord?

ANTIOCHUS.

>Nothing. A sudden and sharp spasm of pain,
>As if the lightning struck me, or the knife
>Of an assassin smote me to the heart.
>'T is passed, even as it came. Let us set forward.

PHILIP.

>See that the chariots be in readiness
>We will depart forthwith.

ANTIOCHUS.

>A moment more.
>I cannot stand. I am become at once
>Weak as an infant. Ye will have to lead me.
>Jove, or Jehovah, or whatever name
>Thou wouldst be named,—it is alike to me,—
>If I knew how to pray, I would entreat
>To live a little longer.

PHILIP.

>O my Lord,
>Thou shalt not die; we will not let thee die!

ANTIOCHUS.

>How canst thou help it, Philip? O the pain!
>Stab after stab. Thou hast no shield against
>This unseen weapon. God of Israel,
>Since all the other gods abandon me,
>Help me. I will release the Holy City.
>Garnish with goodly gifts the Holy Temple.
>Thy people, whom I judged to be unworthy
>To be so much as buried, shall be equal
>Unto the citizens of Antioch.
>I will become a Jew, and will declare

Through all the world that is inhabited
The power of God!

PHILIP.

He faints. It is like death.
Bring here the royal litter. We will bear him
In to the camp, while yet he lives.

ANTIOCHUS.

O Philip,
Into what tribulation am I come!
Alas! I now remember all the evil
That I have done the Jews; and for this cause
These troubles are upon me, and behold
I perish through great grief in a strange land.

PHILIP.

Antiochus! my King!

ANTIOCHUS.

Nay, King no longer.
Take thou my royal robes, my signet-ring,
My crown and sceptre, and deliver them
Unto my son, Antiochus Eupator;
And unto the good Jews, my citizens,
In all my towns, say that their dying monarch
Wisheth them joy, prosperity, and health.
I who, puffed up with pride and arrogance,
Thought all the kingdoms of the earth mine own,
If I would but outstretch my hand and take them,
Meet face to face a greater potentate,
King Death—Epiphanes—the Illustrious!
[Dies.

* * * * *

MICHAEL ANGELO

Michel, piu che mortal, Angel divino.

—ARIOSTO.

Similamente operando all' artista
ch' a l'abito dell' arte e man che trema.

—DANTE, Par. xiii., st. 77.

DEDICATION.

Nothing that is shall perish utterly,
>But perish only to revive again
>In other forms, as clouds restore in rain
>The exhalations of the land and sea.
Men build their houses from the masonry
>Of ruined tombs; the passion and the pain
>Of hearts, that long have ceased to beat, remain
>To throb in hearts that are, or are to be.
So from old chronicles, where sleep in dust
>Names that once filled the world with trumpet tones,
>I build this verse; and flowers of song have thrust
Their roots among the loose disjointed stones,
>Which to this end I fashion as I must.
>Quickened are they that touch the Prophet's bones.

PART FIRST.

I.
PROLOGUE AT ISCHIA

The Castle Terrace. VITTORIA COLONNA, and JULIA
GONZAGA.

VITTORIA.
>Will you then leave me, Julia, and so soon,
>To pace alone this terrace like a ghost?

JULIA.
>To-morrow, dearest.

VITTORIA.

> Do not say to-morrow.
> A whole month of to-morrows were too soon.
> You must not go. You are a part of me.

JULIA.

> I must return to Fondi.

VITTORIA.

> The old castle
> Needs not your presence. No one waits for you.
> Stay one day longer with me. They who go
> Feel not the pain of parting; it is they
> Who stay behind that suffer. I was thinking
> But yesterday how like and how unlike
> Have been, and are, our destinies. Your husband,
> The good Vespasian, an old man, who seemed
> A father to you rather than a husband,
> Died in your arms; but mine, in all the flower
> And promise of his youth, was taken from me
> As by a rushing wind. The breath of battle
> Breathed on him, and I saw his face no more,
> Save as in dreams it haunts me. As our love
> Was for these men, so is our sorrow for them.
> Yours a child's sorrow, smiling through its tears;
> But mine the grief of an impassioned woman,
> Who drank her life up in one draught of love.

JULIA.

> Behold this locket. This is the white hair
> Of my Vespasian. This is the flower-of-love,
> This amaranth, and beneath it the device
> Non moritura. Thus my heart remains
> True to his memory; and the ancient castle,
> Where we have lived together, where he died,
> Is dear to me as Ischia is to you.

VITTORIA.

> I did not mean to chide you.

JULIA.

> Let your heart
> Find, if it can, some poor apology
> For one who is too young, and feels too keenly
> The joy of life, to give up all her days
> To sorrow for the dead. While I am true
> To the remembrance of the man I loved
> And mourn for still, I do not make a show
> Of all the grief I feel, nor live secluded
> And, like Veronica da Gambara,
> Drape my whole house in mourning, and drive forth
> In coach of sable drawn by sable horses,
> As if I were a corpse. Ah, one to-day
> Is worth for me a thousand yesterdays.

VITTORIA.

> Dear Julia! Friendship has its jealousies
> As well as love. Who waits for you at Fondi?

JULIA.

> A friend of mine and yours; a friend and friar.
> You have at Naples your Fra Bernadino;
> And I at Fondi have my Fra Bastiano,
> The famous artist, who has come from Rome
> To paint my portrait. That is not a sin.

VITTORIA.

> Only a vanity.

JULIA.

> He painted yours.

VITTORIA.

> Do not call up to me those days departed
> When I was young, and all was bright about me,
> And the vicissitudes of life were things
> But to be read of in old histories,
> Though as pertaining unto me or mine
> Impossible. Ah, then I dreamed your dreams,

And now, grown older, I look back and see
They were illusions.

JULIA.

Yet without illusions
What would our lives become, what we ourselves?
Dreams or illusions, call them what you will,
They lift us from the commonplace of life
To better things.

VITTORIA.

Are there no brighter dreams,
No higher aspirations, than the wish
To please and to be pleased?

JULIA.

For you there are;
I am no saint; I feel the world we live in
Comes before that which is to be here after,
And must be dealt with first.

VITTORIA.

But in what way?

JULIA.

Let the soft wind that wafts to us the odor
Of orange blossoms, let the laughing sea
And the bright sunshine bathing all the world,
Answer the question.

VITTORIA.

And for whom is meant
This portrait that you speak of?

JULIA.

For my friend
The Cardinal Ippolito.

VITTORIA.
> For him?

JULIA
> Yes, for Ippolito the Magnificent.
> 'T is always flattering to a woman's pride
> To be admired by one whom all admire.

VITTORIA.
> Ah, Julia, she that makes herself a dove
> Is eaten by the hawk. Be on your guard,
> He is a Cardinal; and his adoration
> Should be elsewhere directed.

JULIA.
> You forget
> The horror of that night, when Barbarossa,
> The Moorish corsair, landed on our coast
> To seize me for the Sultan Soliman;
> How in the dead of night, when all were sleeping,
> He scaled the castle wall; how I escaped,
> And in my night-dress, mounting a swift steed,
> Fled to the mountains, and took refuge there
> Among the brigands. Then of all my friends
> The Cardinal Ippolito was first
> To come with his retainers to my rescue.
> Could I refuse the only boon he asked
> At such a time, my portrait?

VITTORIA.
> I have heard
> Strange stories of the splendors of his palace,
> And how, apparelled like a Spanish Prince,
> He rides through Rome with a long retinue
> Of Ethiopians and Numidians
> And Turks and Tartars, in fantastic dresses,
> Making a gallant show. Is this the way
> A Cardinal should live?

JULIA.

He is so young;
Hardly of age, or little more than that;
Beautiful, generous, fond of arts and letters,
A poet, a musician, and a scholar;
Master of many languages, and a player
On many instruments. In Rome, his palace
Is the asylum of all men distinguished
In art or science, and all Florentines
Escaping from the tyranny of his cousin,
Duke Alessandro.

VITTORIA.

I have seen his portrait,
Painted by Titian. You have painted it
In brighter colors.

JULIA.

And my Cardinal,
At Itri, in the courtyard of his palace,
Keeps a tame lion!

VITTORIA.

And so counterfeits
St. Mark, the Evangelist!

JULIA.

Ah, your tame lion
Is Michael Angelo.

VITTORIA.

You speak a name
That always thrills me with a noble sound,
As of a trumpet! Michael Angelo!
A lion all men fear and none can tame;
A man that all men honor, and the model
That all should follow; one who works and prays,
For work is prayer, and consecrates his life
To the sublime ideal of his art,

Till art and life are one; a man who holds
Such place in all men's thoughts, that when they speak
Of great things done, or to be done, his name
Is ever on their lips.

JULIA.

You too can paint
The portrait of your hero, and in colors
Brighter than Titian's; I might warn you also
Against the dangers that beset your path;
But I forbear.

VITTORIA.

If I were made of marble,
Of Fior di Persico or Pavonazzo,
He might admire me: being but flesh and blood,
I am no more to him than other women;
That is, am nothing.

JULIA.

Does he ride through Rome
Upon his little mule, as he was wont,
With his slouched hat, and boots of Cordovan,
As when I saw him last?

VITTORIA.

Pray do not jest.
I cannot couple with his noble name
A trivial word! Look, how the setting sun
Lights up Castel-a-mare and Sorrento,
And changes Capri to a purple cloud!
And there Vesuvius with its plume of smoke,
And the great city stretched upon the shore
As in a dream!

JULIA.

Parthenope the Siren!

VITTORIA.

    And yon long line of lights, those sunlit windows
    Blaze like the torches carried in procession
    To do her honor! It is beautiful!

JULIA.

    I have no heart to feel the beauty of it!
    My feet are weary, pacing up and down
    These level flags, and wearier still my thoughts
    Treading the broken pavement of the Past,
    It is too sad. I will go in and rest,
    And make me ready for to-morrow's journey.

VITTORIA.

    I will go with you; for I would not lose
    One hour of your dear presence. 'T is enough
    Only to be in the same room with you.
    I need not speak to you, nor hear you speak;
    If I but see you, I am satisfied.
    [They go in.

MONOLOGUE: THE LAST JUDGMENT

MICHAEL ANGELO's Studio. He is at work on the cartoon of
    the Last Judgment.

MICHAEL ANGELO.

    Why did the Pope and his ten Cardinals
    Come here to lay this heavy task upon me?
    Were not the paintings on the Sistine ceiling
    Enough for them? They saw the Hebrew leader
    Waiting, and clutching his tempestuous beard,
    But heeded not. The bones of Julius
    Shook in their sepulchre. I heard the sound;
    They only heard the sound of their own voices.

    Are there no other artists here in Rome
    To do this work, that they must needs seek me?

Fra Bastian, my Era Bastian, might have done it;
But he is lost to art. The Papal Seals,
Like leaden weights upon a dead man's eyes,
Press down his lids; and so the burden falls
On Michael Angelo, Chief Architect
And Painter of the Apostolic Palace.
That is the title they cajole me with,
To make me do their work and leave my own;
But having once begun, I turn not back.
Blow, ye bright angels, on your golden trumpets
To the four corners of the earth, and wake
The dead to judgment! Ye recording angels,
Open your books and read? Ye dead awake!
Rise from your graves, drowsy and drugged with death,
As men who suddenly aroused from sleep
Look round amazed, and know not where they are!

In happy hours, when the imagination
Wakes like a wind at midnight, and the soul
Trembles in all its leaves, it is a joy
To be uplifted on its wings, and listen
To the prophetic voices in the air
That call us onward. Then the work we do
Is a delight, and the obedient hand
Never grows weary. But how different is it
En the disconsolate, discouraged hours,
When all the wisdom of the world appears
As trivial as the gossip of a nurse
In a sick-room, and all our work seems useless,

What is it guides my hand, what thoughts possess me,
That I have drawn her face among the angels,
Where she will be hereafter? O sweet dreams,
That through the vacant chambers of my heart
Walk in the silence, as familiar phantoms
Frequent an ancient house, what will ye with me?
'T is said that Emperors write their names in green
When under age, but when of age in purple.
So Love, the greatest Emperor of them all,

Writes his in green at first, but afterwards
In the imperial purple of our blood.
First love or last love,—which of these two passions
Is more omnipotent? Which is more fair,
The star of morning or the evening star?
The sunrise or the sunset of the heart?
The hour when we look forth to the unknown,
And the advancing day consumes the shadows,
Or that when all the landscape of our lives
Lies stretched behind us, and familiar places
Gleam in the distance, and sweet memories
Rise like a tender haze, and magnify
The objects we behold, that soon must vanish?

What matters it to me, whose countenance
Is like the Laocoon's, full of pain; whose forehead
Is a ploughed harvest-field, where three-score years
Have sown in sorrow and have reaped in anguish;
To me, the artisan, to whom all women
Have been as if they were not, or at most
A sudden rush of pigeons in the air,
A flutter of wings, a sound, and then a silence?
I am too old for love; I am too old
To flatter and delude myself with visions
Of never-ending friendship with fair women,
Imaginations, fantasies, illusions,
In which the things that cannot be take shape,
And seem to be, and for the moment are.
[Convent bells ring.

Distant and near and low and loud the bells,
Dominican, Benedictine, and Franciscan,
Jangle and wrangle in their airy towers,
Discordant as the brotherhoods themselves
In their dim cloisters. The descending sun
Seems to caress the city that he loves,
And crowns it with the aureole of a saint.
I will go forth and breathe the air a while.

II.
SAN SILVESTRO

A Chapel in the Church of San Silvestra on Monte Cavallo.

VITTORIA COLONNA, CLAUDIO TOLOMMEI, and others.

VITTORIA.

    Here let us rest a while, until the crowd
    Has left the church. I have already sent
    For Michael Angelo to join us here.

MESSER CLAUDIO.

    After Fra Bernardino's wise discourse
    On the Pauline Epistles, certainly
    Some words of Michael Angelo on Art
    Were not amiss, to bring us back to earth.

MICHAEL ANGELO, at the door.

    How like a Saint or Goddess she appears;
    Diana or Madonna, which I know not!
    In attitude and aspect formed to be
    At once the artist's worship and despair!

VITTORIA.

    Welcome, Maestro. We were waiting for you.

MICHAEL ANGELO.

    I met your messenger upon the way,
    And hastened hither.

VITTORIA.

    It is kind of you
    To come to us, who linger here like gossips
    Wasting the afternoon in idle talk.
    These are all friends of mine and friends of yours.

MICHAEL ANGELO.

If friends of yours, then are they friends of mine.
Pardon me, gentlemen. But when I entered
I saw but the Marchesa.

VITTORIA.

Take this seat
Between me and Ser Claudio Tolommei,
Who still maintains that our Italian tongue
Should be called Tuscan. But for that offence
We will not quarrel with him.

MICHAEL ANGELO.

Eccellenza—

VITTORIA.

Ser Claudio has banished Eccellenza
And all such titles from the Tuscan tongue.

MESSER CLAUDIO.

'T is the abuse of them and not the use
I deprecate.

MICHAEL ANGELO.

The use or the abuse
It matters not. Let them all go together,
As empty phrases and frivolities,
And common as gold-lace upon the collar
Of an obsequious lackey.

VITTORIA.

That may be,
But something of politeness would go with them;
We should lose something of the stately manners
Of the old school.

MESSER CLAUDIO.

Undoubtedly.

VITTORIA.

But that
Is not what occupies my thoughts at present,
Nor why I sent for you, Messer Michele.
It was to counsel me. His Holiness
Has granted me permission, long desired,
To build a convent in this neighborhood,
Where the old tower is standing, from whose top
Nero looked down upon the burning city.

MICHAEL ANGELO.

It is an inspiration!

VITTORIA.

I am doubtful
How I shall build; how large to make the convent,
And which way fronting.

MICHAEL ANGELO.

Ah, to build, to build!
That is the noblest art of all the arts.
Painting and sculpture are but images,
Are merely shadows cast by outward things
On stone or canvas, having in themselves
No separate existence. Architecture,
Existing in itself, and not in seeming
A something it is not, surpasses them
As substance shadow. Long, long years ago,
Standing one morning near the Baths of Titus,
I saw the statue of Laocoon
Rise from its grave of centuries, like a ghost
Writhing in pain; and as it tore away
The knotted serpents from its limbs, I heard,
Or seemed to hear, the cry of agony
From its white, parted lips. And still I marvel
At the three Rhodian artists, by whose hands
This miracle was wrought. Yet he beholds
Far nobler works who looks upon the ruins
Of temples in the Forum here in Rome.

If God should give me power in my old age
To build for Him a temple half as grand
As those were in their glory, I should count
My age more excellent than youth itself,
And all that I have hitherto accomplished
As only vanity.

VITTORIA.

I understand you.
Art is the gift of God, and must be used
Unto His glory. That in art is highest
Which aims at this. When St. Hilarion blessed
The horses of Italicus, they won
The race at Gaza, for his benediction
O'erpowered all magic; and the people shouted
That Christ had conquered Marnas. So that art
Which bears the consecration and the seal
Of holiness upon it will prevail
Over all others. Those few words of yours
Inspire me with new confidence to build.
What think you? The old walls might serve, perhaps,
Some purpose still. The tower can hold the bells.

MICHAEL ANGELO.

If strong enough.

VITTORIA.

If not, it can be strengthened.

MICHAEL ANGELO.

I see no bar nor drawback to this building,
And on our homeward way, if it shall please you,
We may together view the site.

VITTORIA.

I thank you.
I did not venture to request so much.

MICHAEL ANGELO.

> Let us now go to the old walls you spake of,
> Vossignoria—

VITTORIA.

> What, again, Maestro?

MICHAEL ANGELO.

> Pardon me, Messer Claudio, if once more
> I use the ancient courtesies of speech.
> I am too old to change.

III.
CARDINAL IPPOLITO.

A richly furnished apartment in the Palace of CARDINAL IPPOLITO.
Night.

JACOPO NARDI, an old man, alone.

NARDI.

> I am bewildered. These Numidian slaves,
> In strange attire; these endless ante-chambers;
> This lighted hall, with all its golden splendors,
> Pictures, and statues! Can this be the dwelling
> Of a disciple of that lowly Man
> Who had not where to lay his head? These statues
> Are not of Saints; nor is this a Madonna,
> This lovely face, that with such tender eyes
> Looks down upon me from the painted canvas.
> My heart begins to fail me. What can he
> Who lives in boundless luxury at Rome
> Care for the imperilled liberties of Florence,
> Her people, her Republic? Ah, the rich
> Feel not the pangs of banishment. All doors
> Are open to them, and all hands extended,
> The poor alone are outcasts; they who risked
> All they possessed for liberty, and lost;

And wander through the world without a friend,
Sick, comfortless, distressed, unknown, uncared for.

Enter CARDINAL HIPPOLITO, in Spanish cloak and slouched hat.

IPPOLITO.

    I pray you pardon me that I have kept you
    Waiting so long alone.

NARDI.

    I wait to see
    The Cardinal.

IPPOLITO.

    I am the Cardinal.
    And you?

NARDI.

    Jacopo Nardi.

IPPOLITO.

    You are welcome
    I was expecting you. Philippo Strozzi
    Had told me of your coming.

NARDI.

    'T was his son
    That brought me to your door.

IPPOLITO.

    Pray you, be seated.
    You seem astonished at the garb I wear,
    But at my time of life, and with my habits,
    The petticoats of a Cardinal would be—
    Troublesome; I could neither ride nor walk,
    Nor do a thousand things, if I were dressed
    Like an old dowager. It were putting wine
    Young as the young Astyanax into goblets
    As old as Priam.

NARDI.

    Oh, your Eminence
    Knows best what you should wear.

IPPOLITO.

    Dear Messer Nardi,
    You are no stranger to me. I have read
    Your excellent translation of the books
    Of Titus Livius, the historian
    Of Rome, and model of all historians
    That shall come after him. It does you honor;
    But greater honor still the love you bear
    To Florence, our dear country, and whose annals
    I hope your hand will write, in happier days
    Than we now see.

NARDI.

    Your Eminence will pardon
    The lateness of the hour.

IPPOLITO.

    The hours I count not
    As a sun-dial; but am like a clock,
    That tells the time as well by night as day.
    So no excuse. I know what brings you here.
    You come to speak of Florence.

NARDI.

    And her woes.

IPPOLITO.

    The Duke, my cousin, the black Alessandro,
    Whose mother was a Moorish slave, that fed
    The sheep upon Lorenzo's farm, still lives
    And reigns.

NARDI.

    Alas, that such a scourge
    Should fall on such a city!

IPPOLITO.

When he dies,
The Wild Boar in the gardens of Lorenzo,
The beast obscene, should be the monument
Of this bad man.

NARDI.

He walks the streets at night
With revellers, insulting honest men.
No house is sacred from his lusts. The convents
Are turned by him to brothels, and the honor
Of women and all ancient pious customs
Are quite forgotten now. The offices
Of the Priori and Gonfalonieri
Have been abolished. All the magistrates
Are now his creatures. Liberty is dead.
The very memory of all honest living
Is wiped away, and even our Tuscan tongue
Corrupted to a Lombard dialect.

IPPOLITO.

And worst of all his impious hand has broken
The Martinella,—our great battle bell,
That, sounding through three centuries, has led
The Florentines to victory,—lest its voice
Should waken in their souls some memory
Of far-off times of glory.

NARDI.

What a change
Ten little years have made! We all remember
Those better days, when Niccola Capponi,
The Gonfaloniere, from the windows
Of the Old Palace, with the blast of trumpets,
Proclaimed to the inhabitants that Christ
Was chosen King of Florence; and already
Christ is dethroned, and slain, and in his stead
Reigns Lucifer! Alas, alas, for Florence!

IPPOLITO.

    Lilies with lilies, said Savonarola;
    Florence and France! But I say Florence only,
    Or only with the Emperor's hand to help us
    In sweeping out the rubbish.

NARDI.

    Little hope
    Of help is there from him. He has betrothed
    His daughter Margaret to this shameless Duke.
    What hope have we from such an Emperor?

IPPOLITO.

    Baccio Valori and Philippo Strozzi,
    Once the Duke's friends and intimates are with us,
    And Cardinals Salvati and Ridolfi.
    We shall soon see, then, as Valori says,
    Whether the Duke can best spare honest men,
    Or honest men the Duke.

NARDI.

    We have determined
    To send ambassadors to Spain, and lay
    Our griefs before the Emperor, though I fear
    More than I hope.

IPPOLITO.

    The Emperor is busy
    With this new war against the Algerines,
    And has no time to listen to complaints
    From our ambassadors; nor will I trust them,
    But go myself. All is in readiness
    For my departure, and to-morrow morning
    I shall go down to Itri, where I meet
    Dante da Castiglione and some others,
    Republicans and fugitives from Florence,
    And then take ship at Gaeta, and go
    To join the Emperor in his new crusade

Against the Turk. I shall have time enough
And opportunity to plead our cause.

NARDI, rising.

It is an inspiration, and I hail it
As of good omen. May the power that sends it
Bless our beloved country, and restore
Its banished citizens. The soul of Florence
Is now outside its gates. What lies within
Is but a corpse, corrupted and corrupting.
Heaven help us all, I will not tarry longer,
For you have need of rest. Good-night.

IPPOLITO.

Good-night.

Enter FRA SEBASTIANO; Turkish attendants.

IPPOLITO.

Fra Bastiano, how your portly presence
Contrasts with that of the spare Florentine
Who has just left me!

FRA SEBASTIANO.

As we passed each other,
I saw that he was weeping.

IPPOLITO.

Poor old man!

FRA SEBASTIANO.

Who is he?

IPPOLITO.

Jacopo Nardi. A brave soul;
One of the Fuoruseiti, and the best
And noblest of them all; but he has made me
Sad with his sadness. As I look on you
My heart grows lighter. I behold a man

Who lives in an ideal world, apart
From all the rude collisions of our life,
In a calm atmosphere.

FRA SEBASTIANO.
　　　　Your Eminence
Is surely jesting. If you knew the life
Of artists as I know it, you might think
Far otherwise.

IPPOLITO.
　　　　But wherefore should I jest?
The world of art is an ideal world,—
The world I love, and that I fain would live in;
So speak to me of artists and of art,
Of all the painters, sculptors, and musicians
That now illustrate Rome.

FRA SEBASTIANO.
　　　　Of the musicians,
I know but Goudimel, the brave maestro
And chapel-master of his Holiness,
Who trains the Papal choir.

IPPOLITO.
　　　　In church this morning,
I listened to a mass of Goudimel,
Divinely chanted. In the Incarnatus,
In lieu of Latin words, the tenor sang
With infinite tenderness, in plain Italian,
A Neapolitan love-song.

FRA SEBASTIANO.
　　　　You amaze me.
Was it a wanton song?

IPPOLITO.
　　　　Not a divine one.
I am not over-scrupulous, as you know,

In word or deed, yet such a song as that.
Sung by the tenor of the Papal choir,
And in a Papal mass, seemed out of place;
There's something wrong in it.

FRA SEBASTIANO.

There's something wrong
In everything. We cannot make the world
Go right. 'T is not my business to reform
The Papal choir.

IPPOLITO.

Nor mine, thank Heaven.
Then tell me of the artists.

FRA SEBASTIANO.

Naming one
I name them all; for there is only one.
His name is Messer Michael Angelo.
All art and artists of the present day
Centre in him.

IPPOLITO.

You count yourself as nothing!

FRA SEBASTIANO.

Or less than nothing, since I am at best
Only a portrait-painter; one who draws
With greater or less skill, as best he may,
The features of a face.

IPPOLITO.

And you have had
The honor, nay, the glory, of portraying
Julia Gonzaga! Do you count as nothing
A privilege like that? See there the portrait
Rebuking you with its divine expression.
Are you not penitent? He whose skilful hand
Painted that lovely picture has not right

To vilipend the art of portrait-painting.
But what of Michael Angelo?

FRA SEBASTIANO.

But lately
Strolling together down the crowded Corso,
We stopped, well pleased, to see your Eminence
Pass on an Arab steed, a noble creature,
Which Michael Angelo, who is a lover
Of all things beautiful, especially
When they are Arab horses, much admired,
And could not praise enough.

IPPOLITO, to an attendant.

Hassan, to-morrow,
When I am gone, but not till I am gone,—
Be careful about that,—take Barbarossa
To Messer Michael Angelo, the sculptor,
Who lives there at Macello dei Corvi,
Near to the Capitol; and take besides
Some ten mule-loads of provender, and say
Your master sends them to him as a present.

FRA SEBASTIANO.

A princely gift. Though Michael Angelo
Refuses presents from his Holiness,
Yours he will not refuse.

IPPOLITO.

You think him like
Thymoetes, who received the wooden horse
Into the walls of Troy. That book of Virgil
Have I translated in Italian verse,
And shall, some day, when we have leisure for it,
Be pleased to read you. When I speak of Troy
I am reminded of another town
And of a lovelier Helen, our dear Countess
Julia Gonzaga. You remember, surely,

The adventure with the corsair Barbarossa,
And all that followed?

FRA SEBASTIANO.
　　A most strange adventure;
　　A tale as marvellous and full of wonder
　　As any in Boccaccio or Sacchetti;
　　Almost incredible!

IPPOLITO.
　　Were I a painter
　　I should not want a better theme than that:
　　The lovely lady fleeing through the night
　　In wild disorder; and the brigands' camp
　　With the red fire-light on their swarthy faces.
　　Could you not paint it for me?

FRA SEBASTIANO.
　　No, not I.
　　It is not in my line.

IPPOLITO.
　　Then you shall paint
　　The portrait of the corsair, when we bring him
　　A prisoner chained to Naples: for I feel
　　Something like admiration for a man
　　Who dared this strange adventure.

FRA SEBASTIANO.
　　I will do it.
　　But catch the corsair first.

IPPOLITO.
　　You may begin
　　To-morrow with the sword. Hassan, come hither;
　　Bring me the Turkish scimitar that hangs
　　Beneath the picture yonder. Now unsheathe it.
　　'T is a Damascus blade; you see the inscription

In Arabic: La Allah illa Allah,—
There is no God but God.

FRA SEBASTIANO.

How beautiful
In fashion and in finish! It is perfect.
The Arsenal of Venice can not boast
A finer sword.

IPPOLITO.

You like it? It is yours.

FRA SEBASTIANO.

You do not mean it.

IPPOLITO.

I am not a Spaniard,
To say that it is yours and not to mean it.
I have at Itri a whole armory
Full of such weapons. When you paint the portrait
Of Barbarossa, it will be of use.
You have not been rewarded as you should be
For painting the Gonzaga. Throw this bauble
Into the scale, and make the balance equal.
Till then suspend it in your studio;
You artists like such trifles.

FRA SEBASTIANO.

I will keep it
In memory of the donor. Many thanks.

IPPOLITO.

Fra Bastian, I am growing tired of Rome,
The old dead city, with the old dead people;
Priests everywhere, like shadows on a wall,
And morning, noon, and night the ceaseless sound
Of convent bells. I must be gone from here;
Though Ovid somewhere says that Rome is worthy
To be the dwelling-place of all the Gods,

I must be gone from here. To-morrow morning
I start for Itri, and go thence by sea
To join the Emperor, who is making war
Upon the Algerines; perhaps to sink
Some Turkish galleys, and bring back in chains
The famous corsair. Thus would I avenge
The beautiful Gonzaga.

FRA SEBASTIANO.

An achievement
Worthy of Charlemagne, or of Orlando.
Berni and Ariosto both shall add
A canto to their poems, and describe you
As Furioso and Innamorato.
Now I must say good-night.

IPPOLITO.

You must not go;
First you shall sup with me. My seneschal
Giovan Andrea dal Borgo a San Sepolcro,—
I like to give the whole sonorous name,
It sounds so like a verse of the Aeneid,—
Has brought me eels fresh from the Lake of Fondi,
And Lucrine oysters cradled in their shells:
These, with red Fondi wine, the Caecu ban
That Horace speaks of, under a hundred keys
Kept safe, until the heir of Posthumus
Shall stain the pavement with it, make a feast
Fit for Lucullus, or Fra Bastian even;
So we will go to supper, and be merry.

FRA SEBASTIANO.

Beware! I Remember that Bolsena's eels
And Vernage wine once killed a Pope of Rome!

IPPOLITO.

'T was a French Pope; and then so long ago;
Who knows?—perhaps the story is not true.

IV

BORGO DELLE VERGINE AT NAPLES

Room in the Palace of JULIA GONZAGA. Night.

JULIA GONZAGA, GIOVANNI VALDESSO.

JULIA.
>Do not go yet.

VALDESSO.
>The night is far advanced;
>I fear to stay too late, and weary you
>With these discussions.

JULIA.
>I have much to say.
>I speak to you, Valdesso, with that frankness
>Which is the greatest privilege of friendship.—
>Speak as I hardly would to my confessor,
>Such is my confidence in you.

VALDESSO.
>Dear Countess
>If loyalty to friendship be a claim
>Upon your confidence, then I may claim it.

JULIA.
>Then sit again, and listen unto things
>That nearer are to me than life itself.

VALDESSO.
>In all things I am happy to obey you,
>And happiest then when you command me most.

JULIA.
>Laying aside all useless rhetoric,
>That is superfluous between us two,
>I come at once unto the point and say,

You know my outward life, my rank and fortune;
Countess of Fondi, Duchess of Trajetto,
A widow rich and flattered, for whose hand
In marriage princes ask, and ask it only
To be rejected. All the world can offer
Lies at my feet. If I remind you of it,
It is not in the way of idle boasting,
But only to the better understanding
Of what comes after.

VALDESSO.

God hath given you also
Beauty and intellect; and the signal grace
To lead a spotless life amid temptations,
That others yield to.

JULIA.

But the inward life,—
That you know not; 't is known but to myself,
And is to me a mystery and a pain.
A soul disquieted, and ill at ease,
A mind perplexed with doubts and apprehensions,
A heart dissatisfied with all around me,
And with myself, so that sometimes I weep,
Discouraged and disgusted with the world.

VALDESSO.

Whene'er we cross a river at a ford,
If we would pass in safety, we must keep
Our eyes fixed steadfast on the shore beyond,
For if we cast them on the flowing stream,
The head swims with it; so if we would cross
The running flood of things here in the world,
Our souls must not look down, but fix their sight
On the firm land beyond.

JULIA.

I comprehend you.
You think I am too worldly; that my head

Swims with the giddying whirl of life about me.
Is that your meaning?

VALDESSO.

          Yes; your meditations
Are more of this world and its vanities
Than of the world to come.

JULIA.

          Between the two
I am confused.

VALDESSO.

          Yet have I seen you listen
Enraptured when Fra Bernardino preached
Of faith and hope and charity.

JULIA.

          I listen,
But only as to music without meaning.
It moves me for the moment, and I think
How beautiful it is to be a saint,
As dear Vittoria is; but I am weak
And wayward, and I soon fall back again
To my old ways, so very easily.
There are too many week-days for one Sunday.

VALDESSO.

Then take the Sunday with you through the week,
And sweeten with it all the other days.

JULIA.

In part I do so; for to put a stop
To idle tongues, what men might say of me
If I lived all alone here in my palace,
And not from a vocation that I feel
For the monastic life, I now am living
With Sister Caterina at the convent
Of Santa Chiara, and I come here only

On certain days, for my affairs, or visits
Of ceremony, or to be with friends.
For I confess, to live among my friends
Is Paradise to me; my Purgatory
Is living among people I dislike.
And so I pass my life in these two worlds,
This palace and the convent.

VALDESSO.

It was then
The fear of man, and not the love of God,
That led you to this step. Why will you not
Give all your heart to God?

JULIA.

If God commands it,
Wherefore hath He not made me capable
Of doing for Him what I wish to do
As easily as I could offer Him
This jewel from my hand, this gown I wear,
Or aught else that is mine?

VALDESSO.

The hindrance lies
In that original sin, by which all fell.

JULIA.

Ah me, I cannot bring my troubled mind
To wish well to that Adam, our first parent,
Who by his sin lost Paradise for us,
And brought such ills upon us.

VALDESSO.

We ourselves,
When we commit a sin, lose Paradise,
As much as he did. Let us think of this,
And how we may regain it.

JULIA.

Teach me, then,
To harmonize the discord of my life,
And stop the painful jangle of these wires.

VALDESSO.

That is a task impossible, until
You tune your heart-strings to a higher key
Than earthly melodies.

JULIA.

How shall I do it?
Point out to me the way of this perfection,
And I will follow you; for you have made
My soul enamored with it, and I cannot
Rest satisfied until I find it out.
But lead me privately, so that the world
Hear not my steps; I would not give occasion
For talk among the people.

VALDESSO.

Now at last
I understand you fully. Then, what need
Is there for us to beat about the bush?
I know what you desire of me.

JULIA.

What rudeness!
If you already know it, why not tell me?

VALDESSO.

Because I rather wait for you to ask it
With your own lips.

JULIA.

Do me the kindness, then,
To speak without reserve; and with all frankness,
If you divine the truth, will I confess it.

VALDESSO.

> I am content.

JULIA.

> Then speak.

VALDESSO.

> You would be free
> From the vexatious thoughts that come and go
> Through your imagination, and would have me
> Point out some royal road and lady-like
> Which you may walk in, and not wound your feet;
> You would attain to the divine perfection,
> And yet not turn your back upon the world;
> You would possess humility within,
> But not reveal it in your outward actions;
> You would have patience, but without the rude
> Occasions that require its exercise;
> You would despise the world, but in such fashion
> The world should not despise you in return;
> Would clothe the soul with all the Christian graces,
> Yet not despoil the body of its gauds;
> Would feed the soul with spiritual food,
> Yet not deprive the body of its feasts;
> Would seem angelic in the sight of God,
> Yet not too saint-like in the eyes of men;
> In short, would lead a holy Christian life
> In such a way that even your nearest friend
> Would not detect therein one circumstance
> To show a change from what it was before.
> Have I divined your secret?

JULIA.

> You have drawn
> The portrait of my inner self as truly
> As the most skilful painter ever painted
> A human face.

VALDESSO.

> This warrants me in saying
> You think you can win heaven by compromise,
> And not by verdict.

> JULIA
> You have often told me
> That a bad compromise was better even
> Than a good verdict.

VALDESSO.

> Yes, in suits at law;
> Not in religion. With the human soul
> There is no compromise. By faith alone
> Can man be justified.

JULIA.

> Hush, dear Valdesso;
> That is a heresy. Do not, I pray you,
> Proclaim it from the house-top, but preserve it
> As something precious, hidden in your heart,
> As I, who half believe and tremble at it.

VALDESSO.

> I must proclaim the truth.

JULIA.

> Enthusiast!
> Why must you? You imperil both yourself
> And friends by your imprudence. Pray, be patient.
> You have occasion now to show that virtue
> Which you lay stress upon. Let us return
> To our lost pathway. Show me by what steps
> I shall walk in it.
> [Convent bells are heard.

VALDESSO.

> Hark! the convent bells
> Are ringing; it is midnight; I must leave you.

And yet I linger. Pardon me, dear Countess,
Since you to-night have made me your confessor,
If I so far may venture, I will warn you
Upon one point.

JULIA.

What is it? Speak, I pray you,
For I have no concealments in my conduct;
All is as open as the light of day.
What is it you would warn me of?

VALDESSO.

Your friendship
With Cardinal Ippolito.

JULIA.

What is there
To cause suspicion or alarm in that,
More than in friendships that I entertain
With you and others? I ne'er sat with him
Alone at night, as I am sitting now
With you, Valdesso.

VALDESSO.

Pardon me; the portrait
That Fra Bastiano painted was for him.
Is that quite prudent?

JULIA.

That is the same question
Vittoria put to me, when I last saw her.
I make you the same answer. That was not
A pledge of love, but of pure gratitude.
Recall the adventure of that dreadful night
When Barbarossa with two thousand Moors
Landed upon the coast, and in the darkness
Attacked my castle. Then, without delay,
The Cardinal came hurrying down from Rome
To rescue and protect me. Was it wrong

That in an hour like that I did not weigh
Too nicely this or that, but granted him
A boon that pleased him, and that flattered me?

VALDESSO.
Only beware lest, in disguise of friendship
Another corsair, worse than Barbarossa,
Steal in and seize the castle, not by storm
But strategy. And now I take my leave.

JULIA.
Farewell; but ere you go look forth and see
How night hath hushed the clamor and the stir
Of the tumultuous streets. The cloudless moon
Roofs the whole city as with tiles of silver;
The dim, mysterious sea in silence sleeps;
And straight into the air Vesuvius lifts
His plume of smoke. How beautiful it is!
[Voices in the street.

GIOVAN ANDREA.
Poisoned at Itri.

ANOTHER VOICE.
Poisoned? Who is poisoned?

GIOVAN ANDREA.
The Cardinal Ippolito, my master.
Call it malaria. It was sudden.
[Julia swoons.

V.
VITTORIA COLONNA

A room in the Torre Argentina.

VITTORIA COLONNA and JULIA GONZAGA.

VITTORIA.

> Come to my arms and to my heart once more;
> My soul goes out to meet you and embrace you,
> For we are of the sisterhood of sorrow.
> I know what you have suffered.

JULIA.

> Name it not.
> Let me forget it.

VITTORIA.

> I will say no more.
> Let me look at you. What a joy it is
> To see your face, to hear your voice again!
> You bring with you a breath as of the morn,
> A memory of the far-off happy days
> When we were young. When did you come from Fondi?

JULIA.

> I have not been at Fondi since—

VITTORIA.

> Ah me!
> You need not speak the word; I understand you.

JULIA.

> I came from Naples by the lovely valley
> The Terra di Lavoro.

VITTORIA.

> And you find me
> But just returned from a long journey northward.

I have been staying with that noble woman
Renee of France, the Duchess of Ferrara.

JULIA.

Oh, tell me of the Duchess. I have heard
Flaminio speak her praises with such warmth
That I am eager to hear more of her
And of her brilliant court.

VITTORIA.

You shall hear all
But first sit down and listen patiently
While I confess myself.

JULIA.

What deadly sin
Have you committed?

VITTORIA.

Not a sin; a folly
I chid you once at Ischia, when you told me
That brave Fra Bastian was to paint your portrait.

JULIA

Well I remember it.

VITTORIA.

Then chide me now,
For I confess to something still more strange.
Old as I am, I have at last consented
To the entreaties and the supplications
Of Michael Angelo—

JULIA

To marry him?

VITTORIA.

I pray you, do not jest with me! You now,
Or you should know, that never such a thought

Entered my breast. I am already married.
The Marquis of Pescara is my husband,
And death has not divorced us.

JULIA.

Pardon me.
Have I offended you?

VITTORIA.

No, but have hurt me.
Unto my buried lord I give myself,
Unto my friend the shadow of myself,
My portrait. It is not from vanity,
But for the love I bear him.

JULIA.

I rejoice
To hear these words. Oh, this will be a portrait
Worthy of both of you! [A knock.

VITTORIA.

Hark! He is coming.

JULIA.

And shall I go or stay?

VITTORIA.

By all means, stay.
The drawing will be better for your presence;
You will enliven me.

JULIA.

I shall not speak;
The presence of great men doth take from me
All power of speech. I only gaze at them
In silent wonder, as if they were gods,
Or the inhabitants of some other planet.

Enter MICHAEL ANGELO.

VITTORIA.
　　Come in.

MICHAEL ANGELO.
　　I fear my visit is ill-timed;
　　I interrupt you.

VITTORIA.
　　No; this is a friend
　　Of yours as well as mine,—the Lady Julia,
　　The Duchess of Trajetto.

MICHAEL ANGELO to JULIA.
　　I salute you.
　　'T is long since I have seen your face, my lady;
　　Pardon me if I say that having seen it,
　　One never can forget it.

JULIA.
　　You are kind
　　To keep me in your memory.

MICHAEL ANGELO.
　　It is
　　The privilege of age to speak with frankness.
　　You will not be offended when I say
　　That never was your beauty more divine.

JULIA.
　　When Michael Angelo condescends to flatter
　　Or praise me, I am proud, and not offended.

VITTORIA.
　　Now this is gallantry enough for one;
　　Show me a little.

MICHAEL ANGELO.
　　Ah, my gracious lady,
　　You know I have not words to speak your praise.

I think of you in silence. You conceal
Your manifold perfections from all eyes,
And make yourself more saint-like day by day.
And day by day men worship you the wore.
But now your hour of martyrdom has come.
You know why I am here.

VITTORIA.
Ah yes, I know it,
And meet my fate with fortitude. You find me
Surrounded by the labors of your hands:
The Woman of Samaria at the Well,
The Mater Dolorosa, and the Christ
Upon the Cross, beneath which you have written
Those memorable words of Alighieri,
"Men have forgotten how much blood it costs."

MICHAEL ANGELO.
And now I come to add one labor more,
If you will call that labor which is pleasure,
And only pleasure.

VITTORIA.
How shall I be seated?

MICHAEL ANGELO, opening his portfolio.

Just as you are. The light falls well upon you.

VITTORIA.
I am ashamed to steal the time from you
That should be given to the Sistine Chapel.
How does that work go on?

MICHAEL ANGELO, drawing.
But tardily.
Old men work slowly. Brain and hand alike
Are dull and torpid. To die young is best,

And not to be remembered as old men
Tottering about in their decrepitude.

VITTORIA.

My dear Maestro! have you, then, forgotten
The story of Sophocles in his old age?

MICHAEL ANGELO.

What story is it?

VITTORIA.

When his sons accused him,
Before the Areopagus, of dotage,
For all defence, he read there to his Judges
The Tragedy of Oedipus Coloneus,—
The work of his old age.

MICHAEL ANGELO.

'T is an illusion
A fabulous story, that will lead old men
Into a thousand follies and conceits.

VITTORIA.

So you may show to cavilers your painting
Of the Last Judgment in the Sistine Chapel.

MICHAEL ANGELO.

Now you and Lady Julia shall resume
The conversation that I interrupted.

VITTORIA.

It was of no great import; nothing more
Nor less than my late visit to Ferrara,
And what I saw there in the ducal palace.
Will it not interrupt you?

MICHAEL ANGELO.

Not the least.

VITTORIA.

>Well, first, then, of Duke Ercole: a man
>Cold in his manners, and reserved and silent,
>And yet magnificent in all his ways;
>Not hospitable unto new ideas,
>But from state policy, and certain reasons
>Concerning the investiture of the duchy,
>A partisan of Rome, and consequently
>Intolerant of all the new opinions.

JULIA.

>I should not like the Duke. These silent men,
>Who only look and listen, are like wells
>That have no water in them, deep and empty.
>How could the daughter of a king of France
>Wed such a duke?

MICHAEL ANGELO.

>The men that women marry
>And why they marry them, will always be
>A marvel and a mystery to the world.

VITTORIA.

>And then the Duchess,—how shall I describe her,
>Or tell the merits of that happy nature,
>Which pleases most when least it thinks of pleasing?
>Not beautiful, perhaps, in form and feature,
>Yet with an inward beauty, that shines through
>Each look and attitude and word and gesture;
>A kindly grace of manner and behavior,
>A something in her presence and her ways
>That makes her beautiful beyond the reach
>Of mere external beauty; and in heart
>So noble and devoted to the truth,
>And so in sympathy with all who strive
>After the higher life.

JULIA.

> She draws me to her
> As much as her Duke Ercole repels me.

VITTORIA.

> Then the devout and honorable women
> That grace her court, and make it good to be there;
> Francesca Bucyronia, the true-hearted,
> Lavinia della Rovere and the Orsini,
> The Magdalena and the Cherubina,
> And Anne de Parthenai, who sings so sweetly;
> All lovely women, full of noble thoughts
> And aspirations after noble things.

JULIA.

> Boccaccio would have envied you such dames.

VITTORIA.

> No; his Fiammettas and his Philomenas
> Are fitter company for Ser Giovanni;
> I fear he hardly would have comprehended
> The women that I speak of.

MICHAEL ANGELO.

> Yet he wrote
> The story of Griselda. That is something
> To set down in his favor.

VITTORIA.

> With these ladies
> Was a young girl, Olympia Morate,
> Daughter of Fulvio, the learned scholar,
> Famous in all the universities.
> A marvellous child, who at the spinning wheel,
> And in the daily round of household cares,
> Hath learned both Greek and Latin; and is now
> A favorite of the Duchess and companion
> Of Princess Anne. This beautiful young Sappho
> Sometimes recited to us Grecian odes

That she had written, with a voice whose sadness
Thrilled and o'ermastered me, and made me look
Into the future time, and ask myself
What destiny will be hers.

JULIA.

A sad one, surely.
Frost kills the flowers that blossom out of season;
And these precocious intellects portend
A life of sorrow or an early death.

VITTORIA.

About the court were many learned men;
Chilian Sinapius from beyond the Alps,
And Celio Curione, and Manzolli,
The Duke's physician; and a pale young man,
Charles d'Espeville of Geneva, whom the Duchess
Doth much delight to talk with and to read,
For he hath written a book of Institutes
The Duchess greatly praises, though some call it
The Koran of the heretics.

JULIA.

And what poets
Were there to sing you madrigals, and praise
Olympia's eyes and Cherubina's tresses?

VITTORIA.

No; for great Ariosto is no more.
The voice that filled those halls with melody
Has long been hushed in death.

JULIA.

You should have made
A pilgrimage unto the poet's tomb,
And laid a wreath upon it, for the words
He spake of you.

VITTORIA.
> And of yourself no less,
> And of our master, Michael Angelo.

MICHAEL ANGELO.
> Of me?

VITTORIA.
> Have you forgotten that he calls you
> Michael, less man than angel, and divine?
> You are ungrateful.

MICHAEL ANGELO.
> A mere play on words.
> That adjective he wanted for a rhyme,
> To match with Gian Bellino and Urbino.

VITTORIA.
> Bernardo Tasso is no longer there,
> Nor the gay troubadour of Gascony,
> Clement Marot, surnamed by flatterers
> The Prince of Poets and the Poet of Princes,
> Who, being looked upon with much disfavor
> By the Duke Ercole, has fled to Venice.

MICHAEL ANGELO.
> There let him stay with Pietro Aretino,
> The Scourge of Princes, also called Divine.
> The title is so common in our mouths,
> That even the Pifferari of Abruzzi,
> Who play their bag-pipes in the streets of Rome
> At the Epiphany, will bear it soon,
> And will deserve it better than some poets.

VITTORIA.
> What bee hath stung you?

MICHAEL ANGELO.

    One that makes no honey;
    One that comes buzzing in through every window,
    And stabs men with his sting. A bitter thought
    Passed through my mind, but it is gone again;
    I spake too hastily.

JULIA.

    I pray you, show me
    What you have done.

MICHAEL ANGELO.

    Not yet; it is not finished.

PART SECOND

I
MONOLOGUE

A room in MICHAEL ANGELO'S house.

MICHAEL ANGELO.

    Fled to Viterbo, the old Papal city
    Where once an Emperor, humbled in his pride,
    Held the Pope's stirrup, as his Holiness
    Alighted from his mule! A fugitive
    From Cardinal Caraffa's hate, who hurls
    His thunders at the house of the Colonna,
    With endless bitterness!—Among the nuns
    In Santa Catarina's convent hidden,
    Herself in soul a nun! And now she chides me
    For my too frequent letters, that disturb
    Her meditations, and that hinder me
    And keep me from my work; now graciously

She thanks me for the crucifix I sent her,
And says that she will keep it: with one hand
Inflicts a wound, and with the other heals it.
[Reading.
"Profoundly I believed that God would grant you
A supernatural faith to paint this Christ;
I wished for that which I now see fulfilled
So marvellously, exceeding all my wishes.
Nor more could be desired, or even so much.
And greatly I rejoice that you have made
The angel on the right so beautiful;
For the Archangel Michael will place you,
You, Michael Angelo, on that new day
Upon the Lord's right hand! And waiting that,
How can I better serve you than to pray
To this sweet Christ for you, and to beseech you
To hold me altogether yours in all things."

Well, I will write less often, or no more,
But wait her coming. No one born in Rome
Can live elsewhere; but he must pine for Rome,
And must return to it. I, who am born
And bred a Tuscan and a Florentine,
Feel the attraction, and I linger here
As if I were a pebble in the pavement
Trodden by priestly feet. This I endure,
Because I breathe in Rome an atmosphere
Heavy with odors of the laurel leaves
That crowned great heroes of the sword and pen,
In ages past. I feel myself exalted
To walk the streets in which a Virgil walked,
Or Trajan rode in triumph; but far more,
And most of all, because the great Colonna
Breathes the same air I breathe, and is to me
An inspiration. Now that she is gone,
Rome is no longer Rome till she return.
This feeling overmasters me. I know not
If it be love, this strong desire to be
Forever in her presence; but I know

That I, who was the friend of solitude,
And ever was best pleased when most alone,
Now weary grow of my own company.
For the first time old age seems lonely to me.
[Opening the Divina Commedia.
I turn for consolation to the leaves
Of the great master of our Tuscan tongue,
Whose words, like colored garnet-shirls in lava,
Betray the heat in which they were engendered.
A mendicant, he ate the bitter bread
Of others, but repaid their meagre gifts
With immortality. In courts of princes
He was a by-word, and in streets of towns
Was mocked by children, like the Hebrew prophet,
Himself a prophet. I too know the cry,
Go up, thou bald head! from a generation
That, wanting reverence, wanteth the best food
The soul can feed on. There's not room enough
For age and youth upon this little planet.
Age must give way. There was not room enough
Even for this great poet. In his song
I hear reverberate the gates of Florence,
Closing upon him, never more to open;
But mingled with the sound are melodies
Celestial from the gates of paradise.
He came, and he is gone. The people knew not
What manner of man was passing by their doors,
Until he passed no more; but in his vision
He saw the torments and beatitudes
Of souls condemned or pardoned, and hath left
Behind him this sublime Apocalypse.

I strive in vain to draw here on the margin
The face of Beatrice. It is not hers,
But the Colonna's. Each hath his ideal,
The image of some woman excellent,
That is his guide. No Grecian art, nor Roman,
Hath yet revealed such loveliness as hers.

II

VITERBO

VITTORIA COLONNA at the convent window.

VITTORIA.

 Parting with friends is temporary death,
 As all death is. We see no more their faces,
 Nor hear their voices, save in memory;
 But messages of love give us assurance
 That we are not forgotten. Who shall say
 That from the world of spirits comes no greeting,
 No message of remembrance? It may be
 The thoughts that visit us, we know not whence,
 Sudden as inspiration, are the whispers
 Of disembodied spirits, speaking to us
 As friends, who wait outside a prison wall,
 Through the barred windows speak to those within.
 [A pause.

 As quiet as the lake that lies beneath me,
 As quiet as the tranquil sky above me,
 As quiet as a heart that beats no more,
 This convent seems. Above, below, all peace!
 Silence and solitude, the soul's best friends,
 Are with me here, and the tumultuous world
 Makes no more noise than the remotest planet.
 O gentle spirit, unto the third circle
 Of heaven among the blessed souls ascended,
 Who, living in the faith and dying for it,
 Have gone to their reward, I do not sigh
 For thee as being dead, but for myself
 That I am still alive. Turn those dear eyes,
 Once so benignant to me, upon mine,
 That open to their tears such uncontrolled
 And such continual issue. Still awhile
 Have patience; I will come to thee at last.
 A few more goings in and out these doors,
 A few more chimings of these convent bells,

A few more prayers, a few more sighs and tears,
And the long agony of this life will end,
And I shall be with thee. If I am wanting
To thy well-being, as thou art to mine,
Have patience; I will come to thee at last.
Ye minds that loiter in these cloister gardens,
Or wander far above the city walls,
Bear unto him this message, that I ever
Or speak or think of him, or weep for him.

By unseen hands uplifted in the light
Of sunset, yonder solitary cloud
Floats, with its white apparel blown abroad,
And wafted up to heaven. It fades away,
And melts into the air. Ah, would that I
Could thus be wafted unto thee, Francesco,
A cloud of white, an incorporeal spirit!

III
MICHAEL ANGELO AND BENVENUTO CELLINI

MICHAEL ANGELO, BENVENUTO CELLINI in gay attire.

BENVENUTO.
    A good day and good year to the divine
    Maestro Michael Angelo, the sculptor!

MICHAEL ANGELO.
    Welcome, my Benvenuto.

BENVENUTO.
    That is what
    My father said, the first time he beheld
    This handsome face. But say farewell, not welcome.
    I come to take my leave. I start for Florence
    As fast as horse can carry me. I long
    To set once more upon its level flags
    These feet, made sore by your vile Roman pavements.

Come with me; you are wanted there in Florence.
The Sacristy is not finished.

MICHAEL ANGELO.

Speak not of it!
How damp and cold it was! How my bones ached
And my head reeled, when I was working there!
I am too old. I will stay here in Rome,
Where all is old and crumbling, like myself,
To hopeless ruin. All roads lead to Rome.

BENVENUTO.

And all lead out of it.

MICHAEL ANGELO.

There is a charm,
A certain something in the atmosphere,
That all men feel, and no man can describe.

BENVENUTO.

Malaria?

MICHAEL ANGELO.

Yes, malaria of the mind,
Out of this tomb of the majestic Past!
The fever to accomplish some great work
That will not let us sleep. I must go on
Until I die.

BENVENUTO.

Do you ne'er think of Florence?

MICHAEL ANGELO.

Yes; whenever
I think of anything beside my work,
I think of Florence. I remember, too,
The bitter days I passed among the quarries
Of Seravezza and Pietrasanta;
Road-building in the marshes; stupid people,

And cold and rain incessant, and mad gusts
Of mountain wind, like howling dervishes,
That spun and whirled the eddying snow about them
As if it were a garment; aye, vexations
And troubles of all kinds, that ended only
In loss of time and money.

BENVENUTO.
True; Maestro,
But that was not in Florence. You should leave
Such work to others. Sweeter memories
Cluster about you, in the pleasant city
Upon the Arno.

MICHAEL ANGELO.
In my waking dreams
I see the marvellous dome of Brunelleschi,
Ghiberti's gates of bronze, and Giotto's tower;
And Ghirlandajo's lovely Benci glides
With folded hands amid my troubled thoughts,
A splendid vision! Time rides with the old
At a great pace. As travellers on swift steeds
See the near landscape fly and flow behind them,
While the remoter fields and dim horizons
Go with them, and seem wheeling round to meet them,
So in old age things near us slip away,
And distant things go with as. Pleasantly
Come back to me the days when, as a youth,
I walked with Ghirlandajo in the gardens
Of Medici, and saw the antique statues,
The forms august of gods and godlike men,
And the great world of art revealed itself
To my young eyes. Then all that man hath done
Seemed possible to me. Alas! how little
Of all I dreamed of has my hand achieved!

BENVENUTO.
Nay, let the Night and Morning, let Lorenzo
And Julian in the Sacristy at Florence,

Prophets and Sibyls in the Sistine Chapel,
And the Last Judgment answer. Is it finished?

MICHAEL ANGELO.

The work is nearly done. But this Last Judgment
Has been the cause of more vexation to me
Than it will be of honor. Ser Biagio,
Master of ceremonies at the Papal court,
A man punctilious and over nice,
Calls it improper; says that those nude forms,
Showing their nakedness in such shameless fashion,
Are better suited to a common bagnio,
Or wayside wine-shop, than a Papal Chapel.
To punish him I painted him as Minos
And leave him there as master of ceremonies
In the Infernal Regions. What would you
Have done to such a man?

BENVENUTO.

I would have killed him.
When any one insults me, if I can
I kill him, kill him.

MICHAEL ANGELO.

Oh, you gentlemen,
Who dress in silks and velvets, and wear swords,
Are ready with your weapon; and have all
A taste for homicide.

BENVENUTO.

I learned that lesson
Under Pope Clement at the siege of Rome,
Some twenty years ago. As I was standing
Upon the ramparts of the Campo Santo
With Alessandro Bene, I beheld
A sea of fog, that covered all the plain,
And hid from us the foe; when suddenly,
A misty figure, like an apparition,
Rose up above the fog, as if on horseback.

At this I aimed my arquebus, and fired.
The figure vanished; and there rose a cry
Out of the darkness, long and fierce and loud,
With imprecations in all languages.
It was the Constable of France, the Bourbon,
That I had slain.

MICHAEL ANGELO.
Rome should be grateful to you.

BENVENUTO.
But has not been; you shall hear presently.
During the siege I served as bombardier,
There in St. Angelo. His Holiness,
One day, was walking with his Cardinals
On the round bastion, while I stood above
Among my falconets. All thought and feeling,
All skill in art and all desire of fame,
Were swallowed up in the delightful music
Of that artillery. I saw far off,
Within the enemy's trenches on the Prati,
A Spanish cavalier in scarlet cloak;
And firing at him with due aim and range,
I cut the gay Hidalgo in two pieces.
The eyes are dry that wept for him in Spain.
His Holiness, delighted beyond measure
With such display of gunnery, and amazed
To see the man in scarlet cut in two,
Gave me his benediction, and absolved me
From all the homicides I had committed
In service of the Apostolic Church,
Or should commit thereafter. From that day
I have not held in very high esteem
The life of man.

MICHAEL ANGELO.
And who absolved Pope Clement?
Now let us speak of Art.

BENVENUTO.

    Of what you will.

MICHAEL ANGELO.

    Say, have you seen our friend Fra Bastian lately,
    Since by a turn of fortune he became
    Friar of the Signet?

BENVENUTO.

    Faith, a pretty artist
    To pass his days in stamping leaden seals
    On Papal bulls!

MICHAEL ANGELO.

    He has grown fat and lazy,
    As if the lead clung to him like a sinker.
    He paints no more, since he was sent to Fondi
    By Cardinal Ippolito to paint
    The fair Gonzaga. Ah, you should have seen him
    As I did, riding through the city gate,
    In his brown hood, attended by four horsemen,
    Completely armed, to frighten the banditti.
    I think he would have frightened them alone,
    For he was rounder than the O of Giotto.

BENVENUTO.

    He must have looked more like a sack of meal
    Than a great painter.

MICHAEL ANGELO.

    Well, he is not great
    But still I like him greatly. Benvenuto
    Have faith in nothing but in industry.
    Be at it late and early; persevere,
    And work right on through censure and applause,
    Or else abandon Art.

BENVENUTO.

    No man works harder
    Then I do. I am not a moment idle.

MICHAEL ANGELO.

    And what have you to show me?

BENVENUTO.

    This gold ring,
    Made for his Holiness,—my latest work,
    And I am proud of it. A single diamond
    Presented by the Emperor to the Pope.
    Targhetta of Venice set and tinted it;
    I have reset it, and retinted it
    Divinely, as you see. The jewellers
    Say I've surpassed Targhetta.

MICHAEL ANGELO.

    Let me see it.
    A pretty jewel.

BENVENUTO.

    That is not the expression.
    Pretty is not a very pretty word
    To be applied to such a precious stone,
    Given by an Emperor to a Pope, and set
    By Benvenuto!

MICHAEL ANGELO.

    Messer Benvenuto,
    I lose all patience with you; for the gifts
    That God hath given you are of such a kind,
    They should be put to far more noble uses
    Than setting diamonds for the Pope of Rome.
    You can do greater things.

BENVENUTO.

    The God who made me
Knows why he made me what I am,—a goldsmith,
A mere artificer.

MICHAEL ANGELO.

    Oh no; an artist
Richly endowed by nature, but who wraps
His talent in a napkin, and consumes
His life in vanities.

BENVENUTO.

    Michael Angelo
May say what Benvenuto would not bear
From any other man. He speaks the truth.
I know my life is wasted and consumed
In vanities; but I have better hours
And higher aspirations than you think.
Once, when a prisoner at St. Angelo,
Fasting and praying in the midnight darkness,
In a celestial vision I beheld
A crucifix in the sun, of the same substance
As is the sun itself. And since that hour
There is a splendor round about my head,
That may be seen at sunrise and at sunset
Above my shadow on the grass. And now
I know that I am in the grace of God,
And none henceforth can harm me.

MICHAEL ANGELO.

    None but one,—
None but yourself, who are your greatest foe.
He that respects himself is safe from others;
He wears a coat of mail that none can pierce.

BENVENUTO.

    I always wear one.

MICHAEL ANGELO.

O incorrigible!
At least, forget not the celestial vision.
Man must have something higher than himself
To think of.

BENVENUTO.

That I know full well. Now listen.
I have been sent for into France, where grow
The Lilies that illumine heaven and earth,
And carry in mine equipage the model
Of a most marvellous golden salt-cellar
For the king's table; and here in my brain
A statue of Mars Armipotent for the fountain
Of Fontainebleau, colossal, wonderful.
I go a goldsmith, to return a sculptor.
And so farewell, great Master. Think of me
As one who, in the midst of all his follies,
Had also his ambition, and aspired
To better things.

MICHAEL ANGELO.

Do not forget the vision.

[Sitting down again to the Divina Commedia.

Now in what circle of his poem sacred
Would the great Florentine have placed this man?
Whether in Phlegethon, the river of blood,
Or in the fiery belt of Purgatory,
I know not, but most surely not with those
Who walk in leaden cloaks. Though he is one
Whose passions, like a potent alkahest,
Dissolve his better nature, he is not
That despicable thing, a hypocrite;
He doth not cloak his vices, nor deny them.
Come back, my thoughts, from him to Paradise.

IV.
FRA SEBASTIANO DEL PIOMBO

MICHAEL ANGELO; FRA SEBASTIANO DEL PIOMBO.

MICHAEL ANGELO, not turning round.
> Who is it?

FRA SEBASTIANO.
> Wait, for I am out of breath
> In climbing your steep stairs.

MICHAEL ANGELO.
> Ah, my Bastiano,
> If you went up and down as many stairs
> As I do still, and climbed as many ladders,
> It would be better for you. Pray sit down.
> Your idle and luxurious way of living
> Will one day take your breath away entirely.
> And you will never find it.

FRA SEBASTIANO.
> Well, what then?
> That would be better, in my apprehension,
> Than falling from a scaffold.

MICHAEL ANGELO.
> That was nothing
> It did not kill me; only lamed me slightly;
> I am quite well again.

FRA SEBASTIANO.
> But why, dear Master,
> Why do you live so high up in your house,
> When you could live below and have a garden,
> As I do?

MICHAEL ANGELO.
> From this window I can look
> On many gardens; o'er the city roofs
> See the Campagna and the Alban hills;
> And all are mine.

FRA SEBASTIANO.
> Can you sit down in them,
> On summer afternoons, and play the lute
> Or sing, or sleep the time away?

MICHAEL ANGELO.
> I never
> Sleep in the day-time; scarcely sleep at night.
> I have not time. Did you meet Benvenuto
> As you came up the stair?

FRA SEBASTIANO.
> He ran against me
> On the first landing, going at full speed;
> Dressed like the Spanish captain in a play,
> With his long rapier and his short red cloak.
> Why hurry through the world at such a pace?
> Life will not be too long.

MICHAEL ANGELO.
> It is his nature,—
> A restless spirit, that consumes itself
> With useless agitations. He o'erleaps
> The goal he aims at. Patience is a plant
> That grows not in all gardens. You are made
> Of quite another clay.

FRA SEBASTIANO.
> And thank God for it.
> And now, being somewhat rested, I will tell you
> Why I have climbed these formidable stairs.
> I have a friend, Francesco Berni, here,
> A very charming poet and companion,

Who greatly honors you and all your doings,
And you must sup with us.

MICHAEL ANGELO.
    Not I, indeed.
    I know too well what artists' suppers are.
    You must excuse me.

FRA SEBASTIANO.
    I will not excuse you.
    You need repose from your incessant work;
    Some recreation, some bright hours of pleasure.

MICHAEL ANGELO.
    To me, what you and other men call pleasure
    Is only pain. Work is my recreation,
    The play of faculty; a delight like that
    Which a bird feels in flying, or a fish
    In darting through the water,—nothing more.
    I cannot go. The Sibylline leaves of life
    Grow precious now, when only few remain.
    I cannot go.

FRA SEBASTIANO.
    Berni, perhaps, will read
    A canto of the Orlando Inamorato.

MICHAEL ANGELO.
    That is another reason for not going.
    If aught is tedious and intolerable,
    It is a poet reading his own verses,

FRA SEBASTIANO.
    Berni thinks somewhat better of your verses
    Than you of his. He says that you speak things,
    And other poets words. So, pray you, come.

MICHAEL ANGELO.

If it were now the Improvisatore,
Luigia Pulci, whom I used to hear
With Benvenuto, in the streets of Florence,
I might be tempted. I was younger then
And singing in the open air was pleasant.

FRA SEBASTIANO.

There is a Frenchman here, named Rabelais,
Once a Franciscan friar, and now a doctor,
And secretary to the embassy:
A learned man, who speaks all languages,
And wittiest of men; who wrote a book
Of the Adventures of Gargantua,
So full of strange conceits one roars with laughter
At every page; a jovial boon-companion
And lover of much wine. He too is coming.

MICHAEL ANGELO.

Then you will not want me, who am not witty,
And have no sense of mirth, and love not wine.
I should be like a dead man at your banquet.
Why should I seek this Frenchman, Rabelais?
And wherefore go to hear Francesco Berni,
When I have Dante Alighieri here.
The greatest of all poets?

FRA SEBASTIANO.

And the dullest;
And only to be read in episodes.
His day is past. Petrarca is our poet.

MICHAEL ANGELO.

Petrarca is for women and for lovers
And for those soft Abati, who delight
To wander down long garden walks in summer,
Tinkling their little sonnets all day long,
As lap dogs do their bells.

FRA SEBASTIANO.
> I love Petrarca.
> How sweetly of his absent love he sings
> When journeying in the forest of Ardennes!
> "I seem to hear her, hearing the boughs and breezes
> And leaves and birds lamenting, and the waters
> Murmuring flee along the verdant herbage."

MICHAEL ANGELO.
> Enough. It is all seeming, and no being.
> If you would know how a man speaks in earnest,
> Read here this passage, where St. Peter thunders
> In Paradise against degenerate Popes
> And the corruptions of the church, till all
> The heaven about him blushes like a sunset.
> I beg you to take note of what he says
> About the Papal seals, for that concerns
> Your office and yourself.

FRA SEBASTIANO, reading.
> Is this the passage?
> "Nor I be made the figure of a seal
> To privileges venal and mendacious,
> Whereat I often redden and flash with fire!"—
> That is not poetry.

MICHAEL ANGELO.
> What is it, then?

FRA SEBASTIANO.
> Vituperation; gall that might have spirited
> From Aretino's pen.

MICHAEL ANGELO.
> Name not that man!
> A profligate, whom your Francesco Berni
> Describes as having one foot in the brothel
> And the other in the hospital; who lives
> By flattering or maligning, as best serves

His purpose at the time. He writes to me
With easy arrogance of my Last Judgment,
In such familiar tone that one would say
The great event already had occurred,
And he was present, and from observation
Informed me how the picture should be painted.

FRA SEBASTIANO.

What unassuming, unobtrusive men
These critics are! Now, to have Aretino
Aiming his shafts at you brings back to mind
The Gascon archers in the square of Milan,
Shooting their arrows at Duke Sforza's statue,
By Leonardo, and the foolish rabble
Of envious Florentines, that at your David
Threw stones at night. But Aretino praised you.

MICHAEL ANGELO.

His praises were ironical. He knows
How to use words as weapons, and to wound
While seeming to defend. But look, Bastiano,
See how the setting sun lights up that picture!

FRA SEBASTIANO.

My portrait of Vittoria Colonna.

MICHAEL ANGELO.

It makes her look as she will look hereafter,
When she becomes a saint!

FRA SEBASTIANO.

A noble woman!

MICHAEL ANGELO.

Ah, these old hands can fashion fairer shapes
In marble, and can paint diviner pictures,
Since I have known her.

FRA SEBASTIANO.

And you like this picture.
And yet it is in oil; which you detest.

MICHAEL ANGELO.

When that barbarian Jan Van Eyck discovered
The use of oil in painting, he degraded
His art into a handicraft, and made it
Sign-painting, merely, for a country inn
Or wayside wine-shop. 'T is an art for women,
Or for such leisurely and idle people
As you, Fra Bastiano. Nature paints not
In oils, but frescoes the great dome of heaven
With sunset; and the lovely forms of clouds
And flying vapors.

FRA SEBASTIANO.

And how soon they fade!
Behold yon line of roofs and belfries painted
Upon the golden background of the sky,
Like a Byzantine picture, or a portrait
Of Cimabue. See how hard the outline,
Sharp-cut and clear, not rounded into shadow.
Yet that is nature.

MICHAEL ANGELO.

She is always right.
The picture that approaches sculpture nearest
Is the best picture.

FRA SEBASTIANO.

Leonardo thinks
The open air too bright. We ought to paint
As if the sun were shining through a mist.
'T is easier done in oil than in distemper.

MICHAEL ANGELO.

Do not revive again the old dispute;
I have an excellent memory for forgetting,

But I still feel the hurt. Wounds are not healed
By the unbending of the bow that made them.

FRA SEBASTIANO.

So say Petrarca and the ancient proverb.

MICHAEL ANGELO.

But that is past. Now I am angry with you,
Not that you paint in oils, but that grown fat
And indolent, you do not paint at all.

FRA SEBASTIANO.

Why should I paint? Why should I toil and sweat,
Who now am rich enough to live at ease,
And take my pleasure?

MICHAEL ANGELO.

When Pope Leo died,
He who had been so lavish of the wealth
His predecessors left him, who received
A basket of gold-pieces every morning,
Which every night was empty, left behind
Hardly enough to pay his funeral.

FRA SEBASTIANO.

I care for banquets, not for funerals,
As did his Holiness. I have forbidden
All tapers at my burial, and procession
Of priests and friars and monks; and have provided
The cost thereof be given to the poor!

MICHAEL ANGELO.

You have done wisely, but of that I speak not.
Ghiberti left behind him wealth and children;
But who to-day would know that he had lived,
If he had never made those gates of bronze
In the old Baptistery,—those gates of bronze,
Worthy to be the gates of Paradise.
His wealth is scattered to the winds; his children

Are long since dead; but those celestial gates
Survive, and keep his name and memory green.

FRA SEBASTIANO.

But why should I fatigue myself? I think
That all things it is possible to paint
Have been already painted; and if not,
Why, there are painters in the world at present
Who can accomplish more in two short months
Than I could in two years; so it is well
That some one is contented to do nothing,
And leave the field to others.

MICHAEL ANGELO.

O blasphemer!
Not without reason do the people call you
Sebastian del Piombo, for the lead
Of all the Papal bulls is heavy upon you,
And wraps you like a shroud.

FRA SEBASTIANO.

Misericordia!
Sharp is the vinegar of sweet wine, and sharp
The words you speak, because the heart within you
Is sweet unto the core.

MICHAEL ANGELO.

How changed you are
From the Sebastiano I once knew,
When poor, laborious, emulous to excel,
You strove in rivalry with Badassare
And Raphael Sanzio.

FRA SEBASTIANO.

Raphael is dead;
He is but dust and ashes in his grave,
While I am living and enjoying life,
And so am victor. One live Pope is worth
A dozen dead ones.

MICHAEL ANGELO.

    Raphael is not dead;
He doth but sleep; for how can he be dead
Who lives immortal in the hearts of men?
He only drank the precious wine of youth,
The outbreak of the grapes, before the vintage
Was trodden to bitterness by the feet of men.
The gods have given him sleep. We never were
Nor could be foes, although our followers,
Who are distorted shadows of ourselves,
Have striven to make us so; but each one worked
Unconsciously upon the other's thought;
Both giving and receiving. He perchance
Caught strength from me, and I some greater sweetness
And tenderness from his more gentle nature.
I have but words of praise and admiration
For his great genius; and the world is fairer
That he lived in it.

FRA SEBASTIANO.

    We at least are friends;
So come with me.

MICHAEL ANGELO.

    No, no; I am best pleased
When I'm not asked to banquets. I have reached
A time of life when daily walks are shortened,
And even the houses of our dearest friends,
That used to be so near, seem far away.

FRA SEBASTIANO.

    Then we must sup without you. We shall laugh
At those who toil for fame, and make their lives
A tedious martyrdom, that they may live
A little longer in the mouths of men!
And so, good-night.

MICHAEL ANGELO.

    Good-night, my Fra Bastiano.

[*Returning to his work.*

How will men speak of me when I am gone,
When all this colorless, sad life is ended,
And I am dust? They will remember only
The wrinkled forehead, the marred countenance,
The rudeness of my speech, and my rough manners,
And never dream that underneath them all
There was a woman's heart of tenderness.
They will not know the secret of my life,
Locked up in silence, or but vaguely hinted
In uncouth rhymes, that may perchance survive
Some little space in memories of men!
Each one performs his life-work, and then leaves it;
Those that come after him will estimate
His influence on the age in which he lived.

V

PALAZZO BELVEDERE

TITIAN'S studio. A painting of Danae with a curtain before it.

TITIAN, MICHAEL ANGELO, and GIORGIO VASARI.

MICHAEL ANGELO.

So you have left at last your still lagoons,
Your City of Silence floating in the sea,
And come to us in Rome.

TITIAN.

I come to learn,
But I have come too late. I should have seen
Rome in my youth, when all my mind was open
To new impressions. Our Vasari here
Leads me about, a blind man, groping darkly
Among the marvels of the past. I touch them,
But do not see them.

MICHAEL ANGELO.

There are things in Rome
That one might walk bare-footed here from Venice
But to see once, and then to die content.

TITIAN.

I must confess that these majestic ruins
Oppress me with their gloom. I feel as one
Who in the twilight stumbles among tombs,
And cannot read the inscriptions carved upon them.

MICHAEL ANGELO.

I felt so once; but I have grown familiar
With desolation, and it has become
No more a pain to me, but a delight.

TITIAN.

I could not live here. I must have the sea,
And the sea-mist, with sunshine interwoven
Like cloth of gold; must have beneath my windows
The laughter of the waves, and at my door
Their pattering footsteps, or I am not happy.

MICHAEL ANGELO.

Then tell me of your city in the sea,
Paved with red basalt of the Paduan hills.
Tell me of art in Venice. Three great names,
Giorgione, Titian, and the Tintoretto,
Illustrate your Venetian school, and send
A challenge to the world. The first is dead,
But Tintoretto lives.

TITIAN.

And paints with fires
Sudden and splendid, as the lightning paints
The cloudy vault of heaven.

GIORGIO.

    Does he still keep
    Above his door the arrogant inscription
    That once was painted there,—"The color of Titian,
    With the design of Michael Angelo"?

TITIAN.

    Indeed, I know not. 'T was a foolish boast,
    And does no harm to any but himself.
    Perhaps he has grown wiser.

MICHAEL ANGELO.

    When you two
    Are gone, who is there that remains behind
    To seize the pencil falling from your fingers?

GIORGIO.

    Oh there are many hands upraised already
    To clutch at such a prize, which hardly wait
    For death to loose your grasp,—a hundred of them;
    Schiavone, Bonifazio, Campagnola,
    Moretto, and Moroni; who can count them,
    Or measure their ambition?

TITIAN.

    When we are gone
    The generation that comes after us
    Will have far other thoughts than ours. Our ruins
    Will serve to build their palaces or tombs.
    They will possess the world that we think ours,
    And fashion it far otherwise.

MICHAEL ANGELO.

    I hear
    Your son Orazio and your nephew Marco
    Mentioned with honor.

TITIAN.

Ay, brave lads, brave lads.
But time will show. There is a youth in Venice,
One Paul Cagliari, called the Veronese,
Still a mere stripling, but of such rare promise
That we must guard our laurels, or may lose them.

MICHAEL ANGELO.

These are good tidings; for I sometimes fear
That, when we die, with us all art will die.
'T is but a fancy. Nature will provide
Others to take our places. I rejoice
To see the young spring forward in the race,
Eager as we were, and as full of hope
And the sublime audacity of youth.

TITIAN.

Men die and are forgotten. The great world
Goes on the same. Among the myriads
Of men that live, or have lived, or shall live
What is a single life, or thine or mime,
That we should think all nature would stand still
If we were gone? We must make room for others.

MICHAEL ANGELO.

And now, Maestro, pray unveil your picture
Of Danae, of which I hear such praise.

TITIAN, drawing hack the curtain.

What think you?

MICHAEL ANGELO.

That Acrisius did well
To lock such beauty in a brazen tower
And hide it from all eyes.

TITIAN.

> The model truly
> Was beautiful.

MICHAEL ANGELO.

> And more, that you were present,
> And saw the showery Jove from high Olympus
> Descend in all his splendor.

TITIAN.

> From your lips
> Such words are full of sweetness.

MICHAEL ANGELO.

> You have caught
> These golden hues from your Venetian sunsets.

TITIAN.

> Possibly.

MICHAEL ANGELO.

> Or from sunshine through a shower
> On the lagoons, or the broad Adriatic.
> Nature reveals herself in all our arts.
> The pavements and the palaces of cities
> Hint at the nature of the neighboring hills.
> Red lavas from the Euganean quarries
> Of Padua pave your streets; your palaces
> Are the white stones of Istria, and gleam
> Reflected in your waters and your pictures.
> And thus the works of every artist show
> Something of his surroundings and his habits.
> The uttermost that can be reached by color
> Is here accomplished. Warmth and light and softness
> Mingle together. Never yet was flesh
> Painted by hand of artist, dead or living,
> With such divine perfection.

TITIAN.

> I am grateful
> For so much praise from you, who are a master;
> While mostly those who praise and those who blame
> Know nothing of the matter, so that mainly
> Their censure sounds like praise, their praise like censure.

MICHAEL ANGELO.

> Wonderful! wonderful! The charm of color
> Fascinates me the more that in myself
> The gift is wanting. I am not a painter.

GIORGIO.

> Messer Michele, all the arts are yours,
> Not one alone; and therefore I may venture
> To put a question to you.

MICHAEL ANGELO.

> Well, speak on.

GIORGIO.

> Two nephews of the Cardinal Farnese
> Have made me umpire in dispute between them
> Which is the greater of the sister arts,
> Painting or sculpture. Solve for me the doubt.

MICHAEL ANGELO.

> Sculpture and painting have a common goal,
> And whosoever would attain to it,
> Whichever path he take, will find that goal
> Equally hard to reach.

GIORGIO.

> No doubt, no doubt;
> But you evade the question.

MICHAEL ANGELO.

> When I stand
> In presence of this picture, I concede

That painting has attained its uttermost;
But in the presence of my sculptured figures
I feel that my conception soars beyond
All limit I have reached.

GIORGIO.
You still evade me.

MICHAEL ANGELO.
Giorgio Vasari, I have often said
That I account that painting as the best
Which most resembles sculpture. Here before us
We have the proof. Behold those rounded limbs!
How from the canvas they detach themselves,
Till they deceive the eye, and one would say,
It is a statue with a screen behind it!

TITIAN.
Signori, pardon me; but all such questions
Seem to me idle.

MICHAEL ANGELO.
Idle as the wind.
And now, Maestro, I will say once more
How admirable I esteem your work,
And leave you, without further interruption.

TITIAN.
Your friendly visit hath much honored me.

GIOROIO.
Farewell.

MICHAEL ANGELO to GIORGIO, going out.
If the Venetian painters knew
But half as much of drawing as of color,
They would indeed work miracles in art,
And the world see what it hath never seen.

VI
PALAZZO CESARINI

VITTORIA COLONNA, seated in an armchair; JULIA
GONZAGA, standing near her.

JULIA.

    It grieves me that I find you still so weak
    And suffering.

VITTORIA.

    No, not suffering; only dying.
    Death is the chillness that precedes the dawn;
    We shudder for a moment, then awake
    In the broad sunshine of the other life.
    I am a shadow, merely, and these hands,
    These cheeks, these eyes, these tresses that my husband
    Once thought so beautiful, and I was proud of
    Because he thought them so, are faded quite,—
    All beauty gone from them.

JULIA.

    Ah, no, not that.
    Paler you are, but not less beautiful.

VITTORIA.

    Hand me the mirror. I would fain behold
    What change comes o'er our features when we die.
    Thank you. And now sit down beside me here
    How glad I am that you have come to-day,
    Above all other days, and at the hour
    When most I need you!

JULIA.

    Do you ever need me?

VICTORIA.

    Always, and most of all to-day and now.
    Do you remember, Julia, when we walked,

One afternoon, upon the castle terrace
At Ischia, on the day before you left me?

JULIA.

Well I remember; but it seems to me
Something unreal, that has never been,—
Something that I have read of in a book,
Or heard of some one else.

VITTORIA.

Ten years and more
Have passed since then; and many things have happened
In those ten years, and many friends have died:
Marco Flaminio, whom we all admired
And loved as our Catullus; dear Valldesso,
The noble champion of free thought and speech;
And Cardinal Ippolito, your friend.

JULIA.

Oh, do not speak of him! His sudden death
O'ercomes me now, as it o'ercame me then.
Let me forget it; for my memory
Serves me too often as an unkind friend,
And I remember things I would forget,
While I forget the things I would remember.

VITTORIA.

Forgive me; I will speak of him no more,
The good Fra Bernardino has departed,
Has fled from Italy, and crossed the Alps,
Fearing Caraffa's wrath, because he taught
That He who made us all without our help
Could also save us without aid of ours.
Renee of France, the Duchess of Ferrara,
That Lily of the Loire, is bowed by winds
That blow from Rome; Olympia Morata
Banished from court because of this new doctrine.
Therefore be cautious. Keep your secret thought
Locked in your breast.

JULIA.

I will be very prudent
But speak no more, I pray; it wearies you.

VITTORIA.

Yes, I am very weary. Read to me.

JULIA.

Most willingly. What shall I read?

VITTORIA.

Petrarca's
Triumph of Death. The book lies on the table;
Beside the casket there. Read where you find
The leaf turned down. 'T was there I left off reading.

JULIA, reads.

"Not as a flame that by some force is spent,
But one that of itself consumeth quite,
Departed hence in peace the soul content,
In fashion of a soft and lucent light
Whose nutriment by slow gradation goes,
Keeping until the end its lustre bright.
Not pale, but whiter than the sheet of snows
That without wind on some fair hill-top lies,
Her weary body seemed to find repose.
Like a sweet slumber in her lovely eyes,
When now the spirit was no longer there,
Was what is dying called by the unwise.
E'en Death itself in her fair face seemed fair"—

Is it of Laura that he here is speaking?—
She doth not answer, yet is not asleep;
Her eyes are full of light and fixed on something
Above her in the air. I can see naught
Except the painted angels on the ceiling.
Vittoria! speak! What is it? Answer me!—
She only smiles, and stretches out her hands.

[The mirror falls and breaks.

VITTORIA.
>Not disobedient to the heavenly vision!
>Pescara! my Pescara! [Dies.

JULIA.
>Holy Virgin!
>Her body sinks together,—she is dead!

[Kneels and hides her face in Vittoria's lap.

Enter MICHAEL ANGELO.

JULIA.
>Hush! make no noise.

MICHAEL ANGELO.
>How is she?

JULIA.
>Never better.

MICHAEL ANGELO.
>Then she is dead!

JULIA.
>Alas! yes, she is dead!
>Even death itself in her fair face seems fair.
>How wonderful! The light upon her face
>Shines from the windows of another world.
>Saint only have such faces. Holy Angels!
>Bear her like sainted Catherine to her rest!

[Kisses Vittoria's hand.

PART THIRD

I

MONOLOGUE

Macello de' Corvi. A room in MICHAEL ANGELO'S house.
MICHAEL ANGELO, standing before a model of St. Peter's.

MICHAEL ANGELO.

    Better than thou I cannot, Brunelleschi,
    And less than thou I will not! If the thought
    Could, like a windlass, lift the ponderous stones
    And swing them to their places; if a breath
    Could blow this rounded dome into the air,
    As if it were a bubble, and these statues
    Spring at a signal to their sacred stations,
    As sentinels mount guard upon a wall.
    Then were my task completed. Now, alas!
    Naught am I but a Saint Sebaldus, holding
    Upon his hand the model of a church,
    As German artists paint him; and what years,
    What weary years, must drag themselves along,
    Ere this be turned to stone! What hindrances
    Must block the way; what idle interferences
    Of Cardinals and Canons of St. Peter's,
    Who nothing know of art beyond the color
    Of cloaks and stockings, nor of any building
    Save that of their own fortunes! And what then?
    I must then the short-coming of my means
    Piece out by stepping forward, as the Spartan
    Was told to add a step to his short sword.

    [A pause.

    And is Fra Bastian dead? Is all that light
    Gone out, that sunshine darkened; all that music
    And merriment, that used to make our lives

Less melancholy, swallowed up in silence
Like madrigals sung in the street at night
By passing revellers? It is strange indeed
That he should die before me. 'T is against
The laws of nature that the young should die,
And the old live; unless it be that some
Have long been dead who think themselves alive,
Because not buried. Well, what matters it,
Since now that greater light, that was my sun,
Is set, and all is darkness, all is darkness!
Death's lightnings strike to right and left of me,
And, like a ruined wall, the world around me
Crumbles away, and I am left alone.
I have no friends, and want none. My own thoughts
Are now my sole companions,—thoughts of her,
That like a benediction from the skies
Come to me in my solitude and soothe me.
When men are old, the incessant thought of Death
Follows them like their shadow; sits with them
At every meal; sleeps with them when they sleep;
And when they wake already is awake,
And standing by their bedside. Then, what folly
It is in us to make an enemy
Of this importunate follower, not a friend!
To me a friend, and not an enemy,
Has he become since all my friends are dead.

II
VIGNA DI PAPA GIULIO

POPE JULIUS III. seated by the Fountain of Acqua Vergine, surrounded by Cardinals.

JULIUS.
Tell me, why is it ye are discontent,
You, Cardinals Salviati and Marcello,
With Michael Angelo? What has he done,
Or left undone, that ye are set against him?
When one Pope dies, another is soon made;

And I can make a dozen Cardinals,
But cannot make one Michael Angelo.

CARDINAL SALVIATI.

Your Holiness, we are not set against him;
We but deplore his incapacity.
He is too old.

JULIUS.

You, Cardinal Salviati,
Are an old man. Are you incapable?
'T is the old ox that draws the straightest furrow.

CARDINAL MARCELLO.

Your Holiness remembers he was charged
With the repairs upon St. Mary's bridge;
Made cofferdams, and heaped up load on load
Of timber and travertine; and yet for years
The bridge remained unfinished, till we gave it
To Baccio Bigio.

JULIUS.

Always Baccio Bigio!
Is there no other architect on earth?
Was it not he that sometime had in charge
The harbor of Ancona.

CARDINAL MARCELLO.

Ay, the same.

JULIUS.

Then let me tell you that your Baccio Bigio
Did greater damage in a single day
To that fair harbor than the sea had done
Or would do in ten years. And him you think
To put in place of Michael Angelo,
In building the Basilica of St. Peter!
The ass that thinks himself a stag discovers
His error when he comes to leap the ditch.

CARDINAL MARCELLO.

> He does not build; he but demolishes
> The labors of Bramante and San Gallo.

JULIUS.

> Only to build more grandly.

CARDINAL MARCELLO.

> But time passes:
> Year after year goes by, and yet the work
> Is not completed. Michael Angelo
> Is a great sculptor, but no architect.
> His plans are faulty.

JULIUS.

> I have seen his model,
> And have approved it. But here comes the artist.
> Beware of him. He may make Persians of you,
> To carry burdens on your backs forever.

SCENE II.

The same: MICHAEL ANGELO.

JULIUS.

> Come forward, dear Maestro! In these gardens
> All ceremonies of our court are banished.
> Sit down beside me here.

MICHAEL ANGELO, sitting down.

> How graciously
> Your Holiness commiserates old age
> And its infirmities!

JULIUS.

> Say its privileges.
> Art I respect. The building of this palace
> And laying out these pleasant garden walks
> Are my delight, and if I have not asked

Your aid in this, it is that I forbear
To lay new burdens on you at an age
When you need rest. Here I escape from Rome
To be at peace. The tumult of the city
Scarce reaches here.

MICHAEL ANGELO.

How beautiful it is,
And quiet almost as a hermitage!

JULIUS.

We live as hermits here; and from these heights
O'erlook all Rome and see the yellow Tiber
Cleaving in twain the city, like a sword,
As far below there as St. Mary's bridge.
What think you of that bridge?

MICHAEL ANGELO.

I would advise
Your Holiness not to cross it, or not often
It is not safe.

JULIUS.

It was repaired of late.

MICHAEL ANGELO.

Some morning you will look for it in vain;
It will be gone. The current of the river
Is undermining it.

JULIUS.

But you repaired it.

MICHAEL ANGELO.

I strengthened all its piers, and paved its road
With travertine. He who came after me
Removed the stone, and sold it, and filled in
The space with gravel.

JULIUS.

> Cardinal Salviati
> And Cardinal Marcello, do you listen?
> This is your famous Nanni Baccio Bigio.

MICHAEL ANGELO, aside.

> There is some mystery here. These Cardinals
> Stand lowering at me with unfriendly eyes.

JULIUS.

> Now let us come to what concerns us more
> Than bridge or gardens. Some complaints are made
> Concerning the Three Chapels in St. Peter's;
> Certain supposed defects or imperfections,
> You doubtless can explain.

MICHAEL ANGELO.

> This is no longer
> The golden age of art. Men have become
> Iconoclasts and critics. They delight not
> In what an artist does, but set themselves
> To censure what they do not comprehend.
> You will not see them bearing a Madonna
> Of Cimabue to the church in triumph,
> But tearing down the statue of a Pope
> To cast it into cannon. Who are they
> That bring complaints against me?

JULIUS.

> Deputies
> Of the commissioners; and they complain
> Of insufficient light in the Three Chapels.

MICHAEL ANGELO.

> Your Holiness, the insufficient light
> Is somewhere else, and not in the Three Chapels.
> Who are the deputies that make complaint?

JULIUS.
>The Cardinals Salviati and Marcello,
>Here present.

MICHAEL ANGELO, rising.
>With permission, Monsignori,
>What is it ye complain of?

CARDINAL MARCELLO,
>We regret
>You have departed from Bramante's plan,
>And from San Gallo's.

MICHAEL ANGELO.
>Since the ancient time
>No greater architect has lived on earth
>Than Lazzari Bramante. His design,
>Without confusion, simple, clear, well-lighted.
>Merits all praise, and to depart from it
>Would be departing from the truth. San Gallo,
>Building about with columns, took all light
>Out of this plan; left in the choir dark corners
>For infinite ribaldries, and lurking places
>For rogues and robbers; so that when the church
>Was shut at night, not five and twenty men
>Could find them out. It was San Gallo, then,
>That left the church in darkness, and not I.

CARDINAL MARCELLO.
>Excuse me; but in each of the Three Chapels
>Is but a single window.

MICHAEL ANGELO.
>Monsignore,
>Perhaps you do not know that in the vaulting
>Above there are to go three other windows.

CARDINAL SALVIATI.
>How should we know? You never told us of it.

MICHAEL ANGELO.

    I neither am obliged, nor will I be,
To tell your Eminence or any other
What I intend or ought to do. Your office
Is to provide the means, and see that thieves
Do not lay hands upon them. The designs
Must all be left to me.

CARDINAL MARCELLO.

    Sir architect,
You do forget yourself, to speak thus rudely
In presence of his Holiness, and to us
Who are his cardinals.

MICHAEL ANGELO, putting on his hat.

    I do not forget
I am descended from the Counts Canossa,
Linked with the Imperial line, and with Matilda,
Who gave the Church Saint Peter's Patrimony.
I, too, am proud to give unto the Church
The labor of these hands, and what of life
Remains to me. My father Buonarotti
Was Podesta of Chiusi and Caprese.
I am not used to have men speak to me
As if I were a mason, hired to build
A garden wall, and paid on Saturdays
So much an hour.

CARDINAL SALVIATI, aside.

    No wonder that Pope Clement
Never sat down in presence of this man,
Lest he should do the same; and always bade him
Put on his hat, lest he unasked should do it!

MICHAEL ANGELO.

    If any one could die of grief and shame,
I should. This labor was imposed upon me;
I did not seek it; and if I assumed it,
'T was not for love of fame or love of gain,

But for the love of God. Perhaps old age
Deceived me, or self-interest, or ambition;
I may be doing harm instead of good.
Therefore, I pray your Holiness, release me;
Take off from me the burden of this work;
Let me go back to Florence.

JULIUS.

Never, never,
While I am living.

MICHAEL ANGELO.

Doth your Holiness
Remember what the Holy Scriptures say
Of the inevitable time, when those
Who look out of the windows shall be darkened,
And the almond-tree shall flourish?

JULIUS.

That is in
Ecclesiastes.

MICHAEL ANGELO.

And the grasshopper
Shall be a burden, and desire shall fail,
Because man goeth unto his long home.
Vanity of vanities, saith the Preacher; all
Is vanity.

JULIUS.

Ah, were to do a thing
As easy as to dream of doing it,
We should not want for artists. But the men
Who carry out in act their great designs
Are few in number; ay, they may be counted
Upon the fingers of this hand. Your place
Is at St. Peter's.

MICHAEL ANGELO.
>I have had my dream,
>And cannot carry out my great conception,
>And put it into act.

JULIUS.
>Then who can do it?
>You would but leave it to some Baccio Bigio
>To mangle and deface.

MICHAEL ANGELO.
>Rather than that
>I will still bear the burden on my shoulders
>A little longer. If your Holiness
>Will keep the world in order, and will leave
>The building of the church to me, the work
>Will go on better for it. Holy Father,
>If all the labors that I have endured,
>And shall endure, advantage not my soul,
>I am but losing time.

JULIUS, laying his hands on MICHAEL ANGELO'S shoulders.
>You will be gainer
>Both for your soul and body.

MICHAEL ANGELO.
>Not events
>Exasperate me, but the funest conclusions
>I draw from these events; the sure decline
>Of art, and all the meaning of that word:
>All that embellishes and sweetens life,
>And lifts it from the level of low cares
>Into the purer atmosphere of beauty;
>The faith in the Ideal; the inspiration
>That made the canons of the church of Seville
>Say, "Let us build, so that all men hereafter
>Will say that we were madmen." Holy Father,
>I beg permission to retire from here.

JULIUS.

Go; and my benediction be upon you.

[Michael Angelo goes out.

My Cardinals, this Michael Angelo
Must not be dealt with as a common mason.
He comes of noble blood, and for his crest
Bear two bull's horns; and he has given us proof
That he can toss with them. From this day forth
Unto the end of time, let no man utter
The name of Baccio Bigio in my presence.
All great achievements are the natural fruits
Of a great character. As trees bear not
Their fruits of the same size and quality,
But each one in its kind with equal ease,
So are great deeds as natural to great men
As mean things are to small ones. By his work
We know the master. Let us not perplex him.

III
BINDO ALTOVITI

A street in Rome. BINDO ALTOVITI, standing at the door of
his house.

MICHAEL ANGELO, passing.

BINDO.

Good-morning, Messer Michael Angelo!

MICHAEL ANGELO.

Good-morning, Messer Bindo Altoviti!

BINDO.

What brings you forth so early?

MICHAEL ANGELO.

  The same reason
  That keeps you standing sentinel at your door,—
  The air of this delicious summer morning.
  What news have you from Florence?

BINDO.

  Nothing new;
  The same old tale of violence and wrong.
  Since the disastrous day at Monte Murlo,
  When in procession, through San Gallo's gate,
  Bareheaded, clothed in rags, on sorry steeds,
  Philippo Strozzi and the good Valori
  Were led as prisoners down the streets of Florence,
  Amid the shouts of an ungrateful people,
  Hope is no more, and liberty no more.
  Duke Cosimo, the tyrant, reigns supreme.

MICHAEL ANGELO.

  Florence is dead: her houses are but tombs;
  Silence and solitude are in her streets.

BINDO.

  Ah yes; and often I repeat the words
  You wrote upon your statue of the Night,
  There in the Sacristy of San Lorenzo:
  "Grateful to me is sleep; to be of stone
  More grateful, while the wrong and shame endure;
  To see not, feel not, is a benediction;
  Therefore awake me not; oh, speak in whispers."

MICHAEL ANGELO.

  Ah, Messer Bindo, the calamities,
  The fallen fortunes, and the desolation
  Of Florence are to me a tragedy
  Deeper than words, and darker than despair.
  I, who have worshipped freedom from my cradle,
  Have loved her with the passion of a lover,
  And clothed her with all lovely attributes

That the imagination can conceive,
Or the heart conjure up, now see her dead,
And trodden in the dust beneath the feet
Of an adventurer! It is a grief
Too great for me to bear in my old age.

BINDO.
I say no news from Florence: I am wrong,
For Benvenuto writes that he is coming
To be my guest in Rome.

MICHAEL ANGELO.
Those are good tidings.
He hath been many years away from us.

BINDO.
Pray you, come in.

MICHAEL ANGELO.
I have not time to stay,
And yet I will. I see from here your house
Is filled with works of art. That bust in bronze
Is of yourself. Tell me, who is the master
That works in such an admirable way,
And with such power and feeling?

BINDO.
Benvenuto.

MICHAEL ANGELO.
Ah? Benvenuto? 'T is a masterpiece!
It pleases me as much, and even more,
Than the antiques about it; and yet they
Are of the best one sees. But you have placed it
By far too high. The light comes from below,
And injures the expression. Were these windows
Above and not beneath it, then indeed
It would maintain its own among these works
Of the old masters, noble as they are.

I will go in and study it more closely.
I always prophesied that Benvenuto,
With all his follies and fantastic ways,
Would show his genius in some work of art
That would amaze the world, and be a challenge
Unto all other artists of his time.

[They go in.

IV
IN THE COLISEUM

MICHAEL ANGELO and TOMASO DE CAVALIERI

CAVALIERI.
    What have you here alone, Messer Michele?

MICHAEL ANGELO.
    I come to learn.

CAVALIERI.
    You are already master,
    And teach all other men.

MICHAEL ANGELO.
    Nay, I know nothing;
    Not even my own ignorance, as some
    Philosopher hath said. I am a schoolboy
    Who hath not learned his lesson, and who stands
    Ashamed and silent in the awful presence
    Of the great master of antiquity
    Who built these walls cyclopean.

CAVALIERI.
    Gaudentius
    His name was, I remember. His reward
    Was to be thrown alive to the wild beasts
    Here where we now are standing.

MICHAEL ANGELO.
    Idle tales.

CAVALIERI.
    But you are greater than Gaudentius was,
    And your work nobler.

MICHAEL ANGELO.
    Silence, I beseech you.

CAVALIERI.
    Tradition says that fifteen thousand men
    Were toiling for ten years incessantly
    Upon this amphitheatre.

MICHAEL ANGELO.
    Behold
    How wonderful it is! The queen of flowers,
    The marble rose of Rome! Its petals torn
    By wind and rain of thrice five hundred years;
    Its mossy sheath half rent away, and sold
    To ornament our palaces and churches,
    Or to be trodden under feet of man
    Upon the Tiber's bank; yet what remains
    Still opening its fair bosom to the sun,
    And to the constellations that at night
    Hang poised above it like a swarm of bees.

CAVALIERI.
    The rose of Rome, but not of Paradise;
    Not the white rose our Tuscan poet saw,
    With saints for petals. When this rose was perfect
    Its hundred thousand petals were not Saints,
    But senators in their Thessalian caps,
    And all the roaring populace of Rome;
    And even an Empress and the Vestal Virgins,
    Who came to see the gladiators die,
    Could not give sweetness to a rose like this.

MICHAEL ANGELO.

    I spake not of its uses, but its beauty.

CAVALIERI.

    The sand beneath our feet is saturate
    With blood of martyrs; and these rifted stones
    Are awful witnesses against a people
    Whose pleasure was the pain of dying men.

MICHAEL ANGELO.

    Tomaso Cavalieri, on my word,
    You should have been a preacher, not a painter!
    Think you that I approve such cruelties,
    Because I marvel at the architects
    Who built these walls, and curved these noble arches?
    Oh, I am put to shame, when I consider
    How mean our work is, when compared with theirs!
    Look at these walls about us and above us!
    They have been shaken by earthquake; have been made
    A fortress, and been battered by long sieges;
    The iron clamps, that held the stones together,
    Have been wrenched from them; but they stand erect
    And firm, as if they had been hewn and hollowed
    Out of the solid rock, and were a part
    Of the foundations of the world itself.

CAVALIERI.

    Your work, I say again, is nobler work,
    In so far as its end and aim are nobler;
    And this is but a ruin, like the rest.
    Its vaulted passages are made the caverns
    Of robbers, and are haunted by the ghosts
    Of murdered men.

MICHAEL ANGELO.

    A thousand wild flowers bloom
    From every chink, and the birds build their nests
    Among the ruined arches, and suggest
    New thoughts of beauty to the architect,

Now let us climb the broken stairs that lead
Into the corridors above, and study
The marvel and the mystery of that art
In which I am a pupil, not a master.
All things must have an end; the world itself
Must have an end, as in a dream I saw it.
There came a great hand out of heaven, and touched
The earth, and stopped it in its course. The seas
Leaped, a vast cataract, into the abyss;
The forests and the fields slid off, and floated
Like wooded islands in the air. The dead
Were hurled forth from their sepulchres; the living
Were mingled with them, and themselves were dead,—
All being dead; and the fair, shining cities
Dropped out like jewels from a broken crown.
Naught but the core of the great globe remained,
A skeleton of stone. And over it
The wrack of matter drifted like a cloud,
And then recoiled upon itself, and fell
Back on the empty world, that with the weight
Reeled, staggered, righted, and then headlong plunged
Into the darkness, as a ship, when struck
By a great sea, throws off the waves at first
On either side, then settles and goes down
Into the dark abyss, with her dead crew.

CAVALIERI.
    But the earth does not move.

MICHAEL ANGELO.
    Who knows? who knowst?
    There are great truths that pitch their shining tents
    Outside our walls, and though but dimly seen
    In the gray dawn, they will be manifest
    When the light widens into perfect day.
    A certain man, Copernicus by name,
    Sometime professor here in Rome, has whispered
    It is the earth, and not the sun, that moves.
    What I beheld was only in a dream,

Yet dreams sometimes anticipate events,
Being unsubstantial images of things
As yet unseen.

V

MACELLO DE' CORVI

MICHAEL ANGELO, BENVENUTO CELLINI.

MICHAEL ANGELO.

So, Benvenuto, you return once more
To the Eternal City. 'T is the centre
To which all gravitates. One finds no rest
Elsewhere than here. There may be other cities
That please us for a while, but Rome alone
Completely satisfies. It becomes to all
A second native land by predilection,
And not by accident of birth alone.

BENVENUTO.

I am but just arrived, and am now lodging
With Bindo Altoviti. I have been
To kiss the feet of our most Holy Father,
And now am come in haste to kiss the hands
Of my miraculous Master.

MICHAEL ANGELO.

And to find him
Grown very old.

BENVENUTO.

You know that precious stones
Never grow old.

MICHAEL ANGELO.

Half sunk beneath the horizon,
And yet not gone. Twelve years are a long while.
Tell me of France.

BENVENUTO.

> It were too long a tale
> To tell you all. Suffice in brief to say
> The King received me well, and loved me well;
> Gave me the annual pension that before me
> Our Leonardo had, nor more nor less,
> And for my residence the Tour de Nesle,
> Upon the river-side.

MICHAEL ANGELO.

> A princely lodging.

BENVENUTO.

> What in return I did now matters not,
> For there are other things, of greater moment,
> I wish to speak of. First of all, the letter
> You wrote me, not long since, about my bust
> Of Bindo Altoviti, here in Rome. You said,
> "My Benvenuto, I for many years
> Have known you as the greatest of all goldsmiths,
> And now I know you as no less a sculptor."
> Ah, generous Master! How shall I e'er thank you
> For such kind language?

MICHAEL ANGELO.

> By believing it.
> I saw the bust at Messer Bindo's house,
> And thought it worthy of the ancient masters,
> And said so. That is all.

BENVENUTO.

> It is too much;
> And I should stand abashed here in your presence,
> Had I done nothing worthier of your praise
> Than Bindo's bust.

MICHAEL ANGELO.

> What have you done that's better?

BENVENUTO.

> When I left Rome for Paris, you remember
> I promised you that if I went a goldsmith
> I would return a sculptor. I have kept
> The promise I then made.

MICHAEL ANGELO.

> Dear Benvenuto,
> I recognized the latent genius in you,
> But feared your vices.

BENVENUTO.

> I have turned them all
> To virtues. My impatient, wayward nature,
> That made me quick in quarrel, now has served me
> Where meekness could not, and where patience could not,
> As you shall hear now. I have cast in bronze
> A statue of Perseus, holding thus aloft
> In his left hand the head of the Medusa,
> And in his right the sword that severed it;
> His right foot planted on the lifeless corse;
> His face superb and pitiful, with eyes
> Down-looking on the victim of his vengeance.

MICHAEL ANGELO.

> I see it as it should be.

BENVENUTO.

> As it will be
> When it is placed upon the Ducal Square,
> Half-way between your David and the Judith
> Of Donatello.

MICHAEL ANGELO.

> Rival of them both!

BENVENUTO.

> But ah, what infinite trouble have I had
> With Bandinello, and that stupid beast,

The major-domo of Duke Cosimo,
Francesco Ricci, and their wretched agent
Gorini, who came crawling round about me
Like a black spider, with his whining voice
That sounded like the buzz of a mosquito!
Oh, I have wept in utter desperation,
And wished a thousand times I had not left
My Tour do Nesle, nor e'er returned to Florence,
Or thought of Perseus. What malignant falsehoods
They told the Grand Duke, to impede my work,
And make me desperate!

MICHAEL ANGELO.
The nimble lie
Is like the second-hand upon a clock;
We see it fly; while the hour-hand of truth
Seems to stand still, and yet it moves unseen,
And wins at last, for the clock will not strike
Till it has reached the goal.

BENVENUTO.
My obstinacy
Stood me in stead, and helped me to o'ercome
The hindrances that envy and ill-will
Put in my way.

MICHAEL ANGELO.
When anything is done
People see not the patient doing of it,
Nor think how great would be the loss to man
If it had not been done. As in a building
Stone rests on stone, and wanting the foundation
All would be wanting, so in human life
Each action rests on the foregone event,
That made it possible, but is forgotten
And buried in the earth.

BENVENUTO.

> Even Bandinello,
> Who never yet spake well of anything,
> Speaks well of this; and yet he told the Duke
> That, though I cast small figures well enough,
> I never could cast this.

MICHAEL ANGELO.

> But you have done it,
> And proved Ser Bandinello a false prophet.
> That is the wisest way.

BENVENUTO.

> And ah, that casting
> What a wild scene it was, as late at night,
> A night of wind and rain, we heaped the furnace
> With pine of Serristori, till the flames
> Caught in the rafters over us, and threatened
> To send the burning roof upon our heads;
> And from the garden side the wind and rain
> Poured in upon us, and half quenched our fires.
> I was beside myself with desperation.
> A shudder came upon me, then a fever;
> I thought that I was dying, and was forced
> To leave the work-shop, and to throw myself
> Upon my bed, as one who has no hope.
> And as I lay there, a deformed old man
> Appeared before me, and with dismal voice,
> Like one who doth exhort a criminal
> Led forth to death, exclaimed, "Poor Benvenuto,
> Thy work is spoiled! There is no remedy!"
> Then, with a cry so loud it might have reached
> The heaven of fire, I bounded to my feet,
> And rushed back to my workmen. They all stood
> Bewildered and desponding; and I looked
> Into the furnace, and beheld the mass
> Half molten only, and in my despair
> I fed the fire with oak, whose terrible heat
> Soon made the sluggish metal shine and sparkle.

Then followed a bright flash, and an explosion,
As if a thunderbolt had fallen among us.
The covering of the furnace had been rent
Asunder, and the bronze was flowing over;
So that I straightway opened all the sluices
To fill the mould. The metal ran like lava,
Sluggish and heavy; and I sent my workmen
To ransack the whole house, and bring together
My pewter plates and pans, two hundred of them,
And cast them one by one into the furnace
To liquefy the mass, and in a moment
The mould was filled! I fell upon my knees
And thanked the Lord; and then we ate and drank
And went to bed, all hearty and contented.
It was two hours before the break of day.
My fever was quite gone.

MICHAEL ANGELO.
A strange adventure,
That could have happened to no man alive
But you, my Benvenuto.

BENVENUTO.
As my workmen said
To major-domo Ricci afterward,
When he inquired of them: "'T was not a man,
But an express great devil."

MICHAEL ANGELO.
And the statue?

BENVENUTO.
Perfect in every part, save the right foot
Of Perseus, as I had foretold the Duke.
There was just bronze enough to fill the mould;
Not a drop over, not a drop too little.
I looked upon it as a miracle
Wrought by the hand of God.

MICHAEL ANGELO.

> And now I see
> How you have turned your vices into virtues.

BENVENUTO.

> But wherefore do I prate of this? I came
> To speak of other things. Duke Cosimo
> Through me invites you to return to Florence,
> And offers you great honors, even to make you
> One of the Forty-Eight, his Senators.

MICHAEL ANGELO.

> His Senators! That is enough. Since Florence
> Was changed by Clement Seventh from a Republic
> Into a Dukedom, I no longer wish
> To be a Florentine. That dream is ended.
> The Grand Duke Cosimo now reigns supreme;
> All liberty is dead. Ah, woe is me!
> I hoped to see my country rise to heights
> Of happiness and freedom yet unreached
> By other nations, but the climbing wave
> Pauses, lets go its hold, and slides again
> Back to the common level, with a hoarse
> Death rattle in its throat. I am too old
> To hope for better days. I will stay here
> And die in Rome. The very weeds, that grow
> Among the broken fragments of her ruins,
> Are sweeter to me than the garden flowers
> Of other cities; and the desolate ring
> Of the Campagna round about her walls
> Fairer than all the villas that encircle
> The towns of Tuscany.

BENVENUTO.

> But your old friends!

MICHAEL ANGELO.

> All dead by violence. Baccio Valori
> Has been beheaded; Guicciardini poisoned;

Philippo Strozzi strangled in his prison.
Is Florence then a place for honest men
To flourish in? What is there to prevent
My sharing the same fate?

BENVENUTO.
Why this: if all
Your friends are dead, so are your enemies.

MICHAEL ANGELO.
Is Aretino dead?

BENVENUTO.
He lives in Venice,
And not in Florence.

MICHAEL ANGELO.
'T is the same to me
This wretched mountebank, whom flatterers
Call the Divine, as if to make the word
Unpleasant in the mouths of those who speak it
And in the ears of those who hear it, sends me
A letter written for the public eye,
And with such subtle and infernal malice,
I wonder at his wickedness. 'T is he
Is the express great devil, and not you.
Some years ago he told me how to paint
The scenes of the Last Judgment.

BENVENUTO.
I remember.

MICHAEL ANGELO.
Well, now he writes to me that, as a Christian,
He is ashamed of the unbounded freedom
With which I represent it.

BENVENUTO.
Hypocrite!

MICHAEL ANGELO.

    He says I show mankind that I am wanting
    In piety and religion, in proportion
    As I profess perfection in my art.
    Profess perfection? Why, 't is only men
    Like Bugiardini who are satisfied
    With what they do. I never am content,
    But always see the labors of my hand
    Fall short of my conception.

BENVENUTO.

    I perceive
    The malice of this creature. He would taint you
    With heresy, and in a time like this!
    'T is infamous!

MICHAEL ANGELO.

    I represent the angels
    Without their heavenly glory, and the saints
    Without a trace of earthly modesty.

BENVENUTO.

    Incredible audacity!

MICHAEL ANGELO.

    The heathen
    Veiled their Diana with some drapery,
    And when they represented Venus naked
    They made her by her modest attitude,
    Appear half clothed. But I, who am a Christian,
    Do so subordinate belief to art
    That I have made the very violation
    Of modesty in martyrs and in virgins
    A spectacle at which all men would gaze
    With half-averted eyes even in a brothel.

BENVENUTO.

> He is at home there, and he ought to know
> What men avert their eyes from in such places;
> From the Last Judgment chiefly, I imagine.

MICHAEL ANGELO.

> But divine Providence will never leave
> The boldness of my marvellous work unpunished;
> And the more marvellous it is, the more
> 'T is sure to prove the ruin of my fame!
> And finally, if in this composition
> I had pursued the instructions that he gave me
> Concerning heaven and hell and paradise,
> In that same letter, known to all the world,
> Nature would not be forced, as she is now,
> To feel ashamed that she invested me
> With such great talent; that I stand myself
> A very idol in the world of art.
> He taunts me also with the Mausoleum
> Of Julius, still unfinished, for the reason
> That men persuaded the inane old man
> It was of evil augury to build
> His tomb while he was living; and he speaks
> Of heaps of gold this Pope bequeathed to me,
> And calls it robbery;—that is what he says.
> What prompted such a letter?

BENVENUTO.

> Vanity.
> He is a clever writer, and he likes
> To draw his pen, and flourish it in the face
> Of every honest man, as swordsmen do
> Their rapiers on occasion, but to show
> How skilfully they do it. Had you followed
> The advice he gave, or even thanked him for it,
> You would have seen another style of fence.
> 'T is but his wounded vanity, and the wish
> To see his name in print. So give it not
> A moment's thought; it soon will be forgotten.

MICHAEL ANGELO.

> I will not think of it, but let it pass
> For a rude speech thrown at me in the street,
> As boys threw stones at Dante.

BENVENUTO.

> And what answer
> Shall I take back to Grand Duke Cosimo?
> He does not ask your labor or your service;
> Only your presence in the city of Florence,
> With such advice upon his work in hand
> As he may ask, and you may choose to give.

MICHAEL ANGELO.

> You have my answer. Nothing he can offer
> Shall tempt me to leave Rome. My work is here,
> And only here, the building of St. Peter's.
> What other things I hitherto have done
> Have fallen from me, are no longer mine;
> I have passed on beyond them, and have left them
> As milestones on the way. What lies before me,
> That is still mine, and while it is unfinished
> No one shall draw me from it, or persuade me,
> By promises of ease, or wealth, or honor,
> Till I behold the finished dome uprise
> Complete, as now I see it in my thought.

BENVENUTO.

> And will you paint no more?

MICHAEL ANGELO.

> No more.

BENVENUTO.

> 'T is well.
> Sculpture is more divine, and more like Nature,
> That fashions all her works in high relief,
> And that is sculpture. This vast ball, the Earth,
> Was moulded out of clay, and baked in fire;

Men, women, and all animals that breathe
Are statues, and not paintings. Even the plants,
The flowers, the fruits, the grasses, were first sculptured,
And colored later. Painting is a lie,
A shadow merely.

MICHAEL ANGELO.

Truly, as you say,
Sculpture is more than painting. It is greater
To raise the dead to life than to create
Phantoms that seem to live. The most majestic
Of the three sister arts is that which builds;
The eldest of them all, to whom the others
Are but the hand-maids and the servitors,
Being but imitation, not creation.
Henceforth I dedicate myself to her.

BENVENUTO.

And no more from the marble hew those forms
That fill us all with wonder?

MICHAEL ANGELO.

Many statues
Will there be room for in my work. Their station
Already is assigned them in my mind.
But things move slowly. There are hindrances,
Want of material, want of means, delays
And interruptions, endless interference
Of Cardinal Commissioners, and disputes
And jealousies of artists, that annoy me.
But twill persevere until the work
Is wholly finished, or till I sink down
Surprised by death, that unexpected guest,
Who waits for no man's leisure, but steps in,
Unasked and unannounced, to put a stop
To all our occupations and designs.
And then perhaps I may go back to Florence;
This is my answer to Duke Cosimo.

MICHAEL ANGELO'S STUDIO

MICHAEL ANGELO and URBINO.

MICHAEL ANGELO, pausing in his work.
    Urbino, thou and I are both old men.
    My strength begins to fail me.

URBINO.
    Eccellenza.
    That is impossible. Do I not see you
    Attack the marble blocks with the same fury
    As twenty years ago?

MICHAEL ANGELO.
    'T is an old habit.
    I must have learned it early from my nurse
    At Setignano, the stone-mason's wife;
    For the first sounds I heard were of the chisel
    chipping away the stone.

URBINO.
    At every stroke
    You strike fire with your chisel.

MICHAEL ANGELO.
    Ay, because
    The marble is too hard.

URBINO.
    It is a block
    That Topolino sent you from Carrara.
    He is a judge of marble.

MICHAEL ANGELO.
    I remember.
    With it he sent me something of his making,—
    A Mercury, with long body and short legs,

As if by any possibility
A messenger of the gods could have short legs.
It was no more like Mercury than you are,
But rather like those little plaster figures
That peddlers hawk about the villages
As images of saints. But luckily
For Topolino, there are many people
Who see no difference between what is best
And what is only good, or not even good;
So that poor artists stand in their esteem
On the same level with the best, or higher.

URBINO.
How Eccellenza laughed!

MICHAEL ANGELO.
Poor Topolino!
All men are not born artists, nor will labor
E'er make them artists.

URBINO.
No, no more
Than Emperors, or Popes, or Cardinals.
One must be chosen for it. I have been
Your color-grinder six and twenty years,
And am not yet an artist.

MICHAEL ANGELO.
Some have eyes
That see not; but in every block of marble
I see a statue,—see it as distinctly
As if it stood before me shaped and perfect
In attitude and action. I have only
To hew away the stone walls that imprison
The lovely apparition, and reveal it
To other eyes as mine already see it.
But I grow old and weak. What wilt thou do
When I am dead, Urbino?

URBINO.
    Eccellenza,
    I must then serve another master.

MICHAEL ANGELO.
    Never!
    Bitter is servitude at best. Already
    So many years hast thou been serving me;
    But rather as a friend than as a servant.
    We have grown old together. Dost thou think
    So meanly of this Michael Angelo
    As to imagine he would let thee serve,
    When he is free from service? Take this purse,
    Two thousand crowns in gold.

URBINO.
    Two thousand crowns!

MICHAEL ANGELO.
    Ay, it will make thee rich. Thou shalt not die
    A beggar in a hospital.

URBINO.
    Oh, Master!

MICHAEL ANGELO.
    I cannot have them with me on the journey
    That I am undertaking. The last garment
    That men will make for me will have no pockets.

URBINO, kissing the hand of MICHAEL ANGELO.
    My generous master!

MICHAEL ANGELO.
    Hush!

URBINO.
    My Providence!

MICHAEL ANGELO.
Not a word more. Go now to bed, old man.
Thou hast served Michael Angelo. Remember,
Henceforward thou shalt serve no other master.

VII
THE OAKS OF MONTE LUCA

MICHAEL ANGELO, alone in the woods.

MICHAEL ANGELO.
How still it is among these ancient oaks!
Surges and undulations of the air
Uplift the leafy boughs, and let them fall
With scarce a sound. Such sylvan quietudes
Become old age. These huge centennial oaks,
That may have heard in infancy the trumpets
Of Barbarossa's cavalry, deride
Man's brief existence, that with all his strength
He cannot stretch beyond the hundredth year.
This little acorn, turbaned like the Turk,
Which with my foot I spurn, may be an oak
Hereafter, feeding with its bitter mast
The fierce wild boar, and tossing in its arms
The cradled nests of birds, when all the men
That now inhabit this vast universe,
They and their children, and their children's children,
Shall be but dust and mould, and nothing more.
Through openings in the trees I see below me
The valley of Clitumnus, with its farms
And snow-white oxen grazing in the shade
Of the tall poplars on the river's brink.
O Nature, gentle mother, tender nurse!
I who have never loved thee as I ought,
But wasted all my years immured in cities,
And breathed the stifling atmosphere of streets,
Now come to thee for refuge. Here is peace.
Yonder I see the little hermitages
Dotting the mountain side with points of light,

And here St. Julian's convent, like a nest
Of curlews, clinging to some windy cliff.
Beyond the broad, illimitable plain
Down sinks the sun, red as Apollo's quoit,
That, by the envious Zephyr blown aside,
Struck Hyacinthus dead, and stained the earth
With his young blood, that blossomed into flowers.
And now, instead of these fair deities
Dread demons haunt the earth; hermits inhabit
The leafy homes of sylvan Hamadryads;
And jovial friars, rotund and rubicund,
Replace the old Silenus with his ass.

Here underneath these venerable oaks,
Wrinkled and brown and gnarled like them with age,
A brother of the monastery sits,
Lost in his meditations. What may be
The questions that perplex, the hopes that cheer him?
Good-evening, holy father.

MONK.

God be with you.

MICHAEL ANGELO.

Pardon a stranger if he interrupt
Your meditations.

MONK.

It was but a dream,—
The old, old dream, that never will come true;
The dream that all my life I have been dreaming,
And yet is still a dream.

MICHAEL ANGELO.

All men have dreams:
I have had mine; but none of them came true;
They were but vanity. Sometimes I think
The happiness of man lies in pursuing,

Not in possessing; for the things possessed
Lose half their value. Tell me of your dream.

MONK.

The yearning of my heart, my sole desire,
That like the sheaf of Joseph stands up right,
While all the others bend and bow to it;
The passion that torments me, and that breathes
New meaning into the dead forms of prayer,
Is that with mortal eyes I may behold
The Eternal City.

MICHAEL ANGELO.

Rome?

MONK.

There is but one;
The rest are merely names. I think of it
As the Celestial City, paved with gold,
And sentinelled with angels.

MICHAEL ANGELO.

Would it were.
I have just fled from it. It is beleaguered
By Spanish troops, led by the Duke of Alva.

MONK.

But still for me 't is the Celestial City,
And I would see it once before I die.

MICHAEL ANGELO.

Each one must bear his cross.

MONK.

Were it a cross
That had been laid upon me, I could bear it,
Or fall with it. It is a crucifix;
I am nailed hand and foot, and I am dying!

MICHAEL ANGELO.
　What would you see in Rome?

MONK.
　His Holiness.

MICHAEL ANGELO.
　Him that was once the Cardinal Caraffa?
　You would but see a man of fourscore years,
　With sunken eyes, burning like carbuncles,
　Who sits at table with his friends for hours,
　Cursing the Spaniards as a race of Jews
　And miscreant Moors. And with what soldiery
　Think you he now defends the Eternal City?

MONK.
　With legions of bright angels.

MICHAEL ANGELO.
　So he calls them;
　And yet in fact these bright angelic legions
　Are only German Lutherans.

　MONK, crossing himself.
　Heaven protect us?

MICHAEL ANGELO.
　What further would you see?

MONK.
　The Cardinals,
　Going in their gilt coaches to High Mass.

MICHAEL ANGELO.
　Men do not go to Paradise in coaches.

MONK.
　The catacombs, the convents, and the churches;
　The ceremonies of the Holy Week

In all their pomp, or, at the Epiphany,
The Feast of the Santissima Bambino
At Ara Coeli. But I shall not see them.

MICHAEL ANGELO.

These pompous ceremonies of the Church
Are but an empty show to him who knows
The actors in them. Stay here in your convent,
For he who goes to Rome may see too much.
What would you further?

MONK.

I would see the painting
of the Last Judgment in the Sistine Chapel.

MICHAEL ANGELO.

The smoke of incense and of altar candles
Has blackened it already.

MONK.

Woe is me!
Then I would hear Allegri's Miserere,
Sung by the Papal choir.

MICHAEL ANGELO.

A dismal dirge!
I am an old, old man, and I have lived
In Rome for thirty years and more, and know
The jarring of the wheels of that great world,
Its jealousies, its discords, and its strife.
Therefore I say to you, remain content
Here in your convent, here among your woods,
Where only there is peace. Go not to Rome.
There was of old a monk of Wittenberg
Who went to Rome; you may have heard of him;
His name was Luther; and you know what followed.

[The convent bell rings.

MONK, rising.

> It is the convent bell; it rings for vespers.
> Let us go in; we both will pray for peace.

VIII
THE DEAD CHRIST.

MICHAEL ANGELO'S studio. MICHAEL ANGELO, with a
light, working upon the Dead Christ. Midnight.

MICHAEL ANGELO.

> O Death, why is it I cannot portray
> Thy form and features? Do I stand too near thee?
> Or dost thou hold my hand, and draw me back,
> As being thy disciple, not thy master?
> Let him who knows not what old age is like
> Have patience till it comes, and he will know.
> I once had skill to fashion Life and Death
> And Sleep, which is the counterfeit of Death;
> And I remember what Giovanni Strozzi
> Wrote underneath my statue of the Night
> In San Lorenzo, ah, so long ago!
>
> Grateful to me is sleep! More grateful now
> Than it was then; for all my friends are dead;
> And she is dead, the noblest of them all.
> I saw her face, when the great sculptor Death,
> Whom men should call Divine, had at a blow
> Stricken her into marble; and I kissed
> Her cold white hand. What was it held me back
> From kissing her fair forehead, and those lips,
> Those dead, dumb lips? Grateful to me is sleep!

Enter GIORGIO VASARI.

GIORGIO.

> Good-evening, or good-morning, for I know not
> Which of the two it is.

MICHAEL ANGELO.

> How came you in?

GIORGIO.

> Why, by the door, as all men do.

MICHAEL ANGELO.

> Ascanio
> Must have forgotten to bolt it.

GIORGIO.

> Probably.
> Am I a spirit, or so like a spirit,
> That I could slip through bolted door or window?
> As I was passing down the street, I saw
> A glimmer of light, and heard the well-known chink
> Of chisel upon marble. So I entered,
> To see what keeps you from your bed so late.

MICHAEL ANGELO, coming forward with the lamp.

> You have been revelling with your boon companions,
> Giorgio Vasari, and you come to me
> At an untimely hour.

GIORGIO.

> The Pope hath sent me.
> His Holiness desires to see again
> The drawing you once showed him of the dome
> Of the Basilica.

MICHAEL ANGELO.

> We will look for it.

GIORGIO.

> What is the marble group that glimmers there
> Behind you?

MICHAEL ANGELO.

> Nothing, and yet everything,—
> As one may take it. It is my own tomb,
> That I am building.

GIORGIO.

> Do not hide it from me.
> By our long friendship and the love I bear you,
> Refuse me not!

MICHAEL ANGELO, letting fall the lamp.

> Life hath become to me
> An empty theatre,—its lights extinguished,
> The music silent, and the actors gone;
> And I alone sit musing on the scenes
> That once have been. I am so old that Death
> Oft plucks me by the cloak, to come with him
> And some day, like this lamp, shall I fall down,
> And my last spark of life will be extinguished.
> Ah me! ah me! what darkness of despair!
> So near to death, and yet so far from God!

* * * * *

TRANSLATIONS

PRELUDE

As treasures that men seek,
   Deep-buried in sea-sands,
Vanish if they but speak,
   And elude their eager hands,

So ye escape and slip,
   O songs, and fade away,
When the word is on my lip
   To interpret what ye say.

Were it not better, then,
   To let the treasures rest
Hid from the eyes of men,
   Locked in their iron chest?

I have but marked the place,
   But half the secret told,
That, following this slight trace,
   Others may find the gold.

FROM THE SPANISH

COPLAS DE MANRIQUE.

O let the soul her slumbers break,
Let thought be quickened, and awake;
Awake to see
How soon this life is past and gone,
And death comes softly stealing on,
How silently!

Swiftly our pleasures glide away,
Our hearts recall the distant day
With many sighs;
The moments that are speeding fast
We heed not, but the past,—the past,
More highly prize.

Onward its course the present keeps,
Onward the constant current sweeps,
Till life is done;
And, did we judge of time aright,
The past and future in their flight
Would be as one.

Let no one fondly dream again,
That Hope and all her shadowy train
Will not decay;
Fleeting as were the dreams of old,
Remembered like a tale that's told,
They pass away.

Our lives are rivers, gliding free
To that unfathomed, boundless sea,
The silent grave!
Thither all earthly pomp and boast

Roll, to be swallowed up and lost
In one dark wave.

Thither the mighty torrents stray,
Thither the brook pursues its way,
And tinkling rill,
There all are equal; side by side
The poor man and the son of pride
Lie calm and still.

I will not here invoke the throng
Of orators and sons of song,
The deathless few;
Fiction entices and deceives,
And, sprinkled o'er her fragrant leaves,
Lies poisonous dew.

To One alone my thoughts arise,
The Eternal Truth, the Good and Wise,
To Him I cry,
Who shared on earth our common lot,
But the world comprehended not
His deity.

This world is but the rugged road
Which leads us to the bright abode
Of peace above;
So let us choose that narrow way,
Which leads no traveller's foot astray
From realms of love,

Our cradle is the starting-place,
Life is the running of the race,
We reach the goal
When, in the mansions of the blest,
Death leaves to its eternal rest
The weary soul.

Did we but use it as we ought,
This world would school each wandering thought
To its high state.
Faith wings the soul beyond the sky,
Up to that better world on high,
For which we wait.

Yes, the glad messenger of love,
To guide us to our home above,
The Saviour came;
Born amid mortal cares and fears.
He suffered in this vale of tears
A death of shame.

Behold of what delusive worth
The bubbles we pursue on earth,
The shapes we chase,
Amid a world of treachery!
They vanish ere death shuts the eye,
And leave no trace.

Time steals them from us, chances strange,
Disastrous accident, and change,
That come to all;
Even in the most exalted state,
Relentless sweeps the stroke of fate;
The strongest fall.

Tell me, the charms that lovers seek
In the clear eye and blushing cheek,
The hues that play
O'er rosy lip and brow of snow,
When hoary age approaches slow,
Ah; where are they?

The cunning skill, the curious arts,
The glorious strength that youth imparts
In life's first stage;
These shall become a heavy weight,

When Time swings wide his outward gate
To weary age.

The noble blood of Gothic name,
Heroes emblazoned high to fame,
In long array;
How, in the onward course of time,
The landmarks of that race sublime
Were swept away!

Some, the degraded slaves of lust,
Prostrate and trampled in the dust,
Shall rise no more;
Others, by guilt and crime, maintain
The scutcheon, that without a stain,
Their fathers bore.

Wealth and the high estate of pride,
With what untimely speed they glide,
How soon depart!
Bid not the shadowy phantoms stay,
The vassals of a mistress they,
Of fickle heart.

These gifts in Fortune's hands are found;
Her swift revolving wheel turns round,
And they are gone!
No rest the inconstant goddess knows,
But changing, and without repose,
Still hurries on.

Even could the hand of avarice save
Its gilded baubles till the grave
Reclaimed its prey,
Let none on such poor hopes rely;
Life, like an empty dream, flits by,
And where are they?

Earthly desires and sensual lust
Are passions springing from the dust,
They fade and die;
But in the life beyond the tomb,
They seal the immortal spirits doom
Eternally!

The pleasures and delights, which mask
In treacherous smiles life's serious task,
What are they, all,
But the fleet coursers of the chase,
And death an ambush in the race,
Wherein we fall?

No foe, no dangerous pass, we heed,
Brook no delay, but onward speed
With loosened rein;
And, when the fatal snare is near,
We strive to check our mad career,
But strive in vain.

Could we new charms to age impart,
And fashion with a cunning art
The human face,
As we can clothe the soul with light,
And make the glorious spirit bright
With heavenly grace,

How busily each passing hour
Should we exert that magic power,
What ardor show,
To deck the sensual slave of sin,
Yet leave the freeborn soul within,
In weeds of woe!

Monarchs, the powerful and the strong,
Famous in history and in song
Of olden time,
Saw, by the stern decrees of fate,

Their kingdoms lost, and desolate
Their race sublime.

Who is the champion? who the strong?
Pontiff and priest, and sceptred throng?
On these shall fall
As heavily the hand of Death,
As when it stays the shepherd's breath
Beside his stall.

I speak not of the Trojan name,
Neither its glory nor its shame
Has met our eyes;
Nor of Rome's great and glorious dead,
Though we have heard so oft, and read,
Their histories.

Little avails it now to know
Of ages passed so long ago,
Nor how they rolled;
Our theme shall be of yesterday,
Which to oblivion sweeps away,
Like day's of old.

Where is the King, Don Juan? Where
Each royal prince and noble heir
Of Aragon?
Where are the courtly gallantries?
The deeds of love and high emprise,
In battle done?

Tourney and joust, that charmed the eye,
And scarf, and gorgeous panoply,
And nodding plume,
What were they but a pageant scene?
What but the garlands, gay and green,
That deck the tomb?

Where are the high-born dames, and where
Their gay attire, and jewelled hair,
And odors sweet?
Where are the gentle knights, that came
To kneel, and breathe love's ardent flame,
Low at their feet?

Where is the song of Troubadour?
Where are the lute and gay tambour
They loved of yore?
Where is the mazy dance of old,
The flowing robes, inwrought with gold,
The dancers wore?

And he who next the sceptre swayed,
Henry, whose royal court displayed
Such power and pride;
O, in what winning smiles arrayed,
The world its various pleasures laid
His throne beside!

But O how false and full of guile
That world, which wore so soft a smile
But to betray!
She, that had been his friend before,
Now from the fated monarch tore
Her charms away.

The countless gifts, the stately walls,
The loyal palaces, and halls
All filled with gold;
Plate with armorial bearings wrought,
Chambers with ample treasures fraught
Of wealth untold;

The noble steeds, and harness bright,
And gallant lord, and stalwart knight,
In rich array,
Where shall we seek them now? Alas!

Like the bright dewdrops on the grass,
They passed away.

His brother, too, whose factious zeal
Usurped the sceptre of Castile,
Unskilled to reign;
What a gay, brilliant court had he,
When all the flower of chivalry
Was in his train!

But he was mortal; and the breath,
That flamed from the hot forge of Death,
Blasted his years;
Judgment of God! that flame by thee,
When raging fierce and fearfully,
Was quenched in tears!

Spain's haughty Constable, the true
And gallant Master, whom we knew
Most loved of all;
Breathe not a whisper of his pride,
He on the gloomy scaffold died,
Ignoble fall!

The countless treasures of his care,
His villages and villas fair,
His mighty power,
What were they all but grief and shame,
Tears and a broken heart, when came
The parting hour?

His other brothers, proud and high,
Masters, who, in prosperity,
Might rival kings;
Who made the bravest and the best
The bondsmen of their high behest,
Their underlings;

What was their prosperous estate,
When high exalted and elate
With power and pride?
What, but a transient gleam of light,
A flame, which, glaring at its height,
Grew dim and died?

So many a duke of royal name,
Marquis and count of spotless fame,
And baron brave,
That might the sword of empire wield,
All these, O Death, hast thou concealed
In the dark grave!

Their deeds of mercy and of arms,
In peaceful days, or war's alarms,
When thou dost show.
O Death, thy stern and angry face,
One stroke of thy all-powerful mace
Can overthrow.

Unnumbered hosts, that threaten nigh,
Pennon and standard flaunting high,
And flag displayed;
High battlements intrenched around,
Bastion, and moated wall, and mound,
And palisade,

And covered trench, secure and deep,
All these cannot one victim keep,
O Death, from thee,
When thou dost battle in thy wrath,
And thy strong shafts pursue their path
Unerringly.

O World! so few the years we live,
Would that the life which thou dost give
Were life indeed!
Alas! thy sorrows fall so fast,

Our happiest hour is when at last
The soul is freed.

Our days are covered o'er with grief,
And sorrows neither few nor brief
Veil all in gloom;
Left desolate of real good,
Within this cheerless solitude
No pleasures bloom.

Thy pilgrimage begins in tears,
And ends in bitter doubts and fears,
Or dark despair;
Midway so many toils appear,
That he who lingers longest here
Knows most of care.

Thy goods are bought with many a groan,
By the hot sweat of toil alone,
And weary hearts;
Fleet-footed is the approach of woe,
But with a lingering step and slow
Its form departs.

And he, the good man's shield and shade,
To whom all hearts their homage paid,
As Virtue's son,
Roderic Manrique, he whose name
Is written on the scroll of Fame,
Spain's champion;

His signal deeds and prowess high
Demand no pompous eulogy.
Ye saw his deeds!
Why should their praise in verse be sung?
The name, that dwells on every tongue,
No minstrel needs.

To friends a friend; how kind to all
The vassals of this ancient hall
And feudal fief!
To foes how stern a foe was he!
And to the valiant and the free
How brave a chief!

What prudence with the old and wise:
What grace in youthful gayeties;
In all how sage!
Benignant to the serf and slave,
He showed the base and falsely brave
A lion's rage.

His was Octavian's prosperous star,
The rush of Caesar's conquering car
At battle's call;
His, Scipio's virtue; his, the skill
And the indomitable will
Of Hannibal.

His was a Trajan's goodness, his
A Titus' noble charities
And righteous laws;
The arm of Hector, and the might
Of Tully, to maintain the right
In truth's just cause;

The clemency of Antonine,
Aurelius' countenance divine,
Firm, gentle, still;
The eloquence of Adrian,
And Theodosius' love to man,
And generous will;

In tented field and bloody fray,
An Alexander's vigorous sway
And stern command;
The faith of Constantine; ay, more,

The fervent love Camillus bore
His native land.

He left no well-filled treasury,
He heaped no pile of riches high,
Nor massive plate;
He fought the Moors, and, in their fall,
City and tower and castled wall
Were his estate.

Upon the hard-fought battle-ground,
Brave steeds and gallant riders found
A common grave;
And there the warrior's hand did gain
The rents, and the long vassal train,
That conquest gave.

And if, of old, his halls displayed
The honored and exalted grade
His worth had gained,
So, in the dark, disastrous hour,
Brothers and bondsmen of his power
His hand sustained.

After high deeds, not left untold,
In the stern warfare, which of old
'T was his to share,
Such noble leagues he made, that more
And fairer regions, than before,
His guerdon were.

These are the records, half effaced,
Which, with the hand of youth, he traced
On history's page;
But with fresh victories he drew
Each fading character anew
In his old age.

By his unrivalled skill, by great
And veteran service to the state,
By worth adored,
He stood, in his high dignity,
The proudest knight of chivalry,
Knight of the Sword.

He found his cities and domains
Beneath a tyrant's galling chains
And cruel power;
But by fierce battle and blockade,
Soon his own banner was displayed
From every tower.

By the tried valor of his hand,
His monarch and his native land
Were nobly served;
Let Portugal repeat the story,
And proud Castile, who shared the glory
His arms deserved.

And when so oft, for weal or woe,
His life upon the fatal throw
Had been cast down;
When he had served, with patriot zeal,
Beneath the banner of Castile,
His sovereign's crown;

And done such deeds of valor strong,
That neither history nor song
Can count them all;
Then, on Ocana's castled rock,
Death at his portal came to knock,
With sudden call,

Saying, "Good Cavalier, prepare
To leave this world of toil and care
With joyful mien;
Let thy strong heart of steel this day

Put on its armor for the fray,
The closing scene.

"Since thou hast been, in battle-strife,
So prodigal of health and life,
For earthly fame,
Let virtue nerve thy heart again;
Loud on the last stern battle-plain
They call thy name.

"Think not the struggle that draws near
Too terrible for man, nor fear
To meet the foe;
Nor let thy noble spirit grieve,
Its life of glorious fame to leave
On earth below.

"A life of honor and of worth
Has no eternity on earth,
'T is but a name;
And yet its glory far exceeds
That base and sensual life, which leads
To want and shame.

"The eternal life, beyond the sky,
Wealth cannot purchase, nor the high
And proud estate;
The soul in dalliance laid, the spirit
Corrupt with sin, shall not inherit
A joy so great.

"But the good monk, in cloistered cell,
Shall gain it by his book and bell,
His prayers and tears;
And the brave knight, whose arm endures
Fierce battle, and against the Moors
His standard rears.

"And thou, brave knight, whose hand has poured
The life-blood of the Pagan horde
O'er all the land,
In heaven shalt thou receive, at length,
The guerdon of thine earthly strength
And dauntless hand.

"Cheered onward by this promise sure,
Strong in the faith entire and pure
Thou dost profess,
Depart, thy hope is certainty,
The third, the better life on high
Shalt thou possess."

"O Death, no more, no more delay;
My spirit longs to flee away,
And be at rest;
The will of Heaven my will shall be,
I bow to the divine decree,
To God's behest.

"My soul is ready to depart,
No thought rebels, the obedient heart
Breathes forth no sigh;
The wish on earth to linger still
Were vain, when 't is God's sovereign will
That we shall die.

"O thou, that for our sins didst take
A human form, and humbly make
Thy home on earth;
Thou, that to thy divinity
A human nature didst ally
By mortal birth,

"And in that form didst suffer here
Torment, and agony, and fear,
So patiently;
By thy redeeming grace alone,

And not for merits of my own,
O, pardon me!"

As thus the dying warrior prayed,
Without one gathering mist or shade
Upon his mind;
Encircled by his family,
Watched by affection's gentle eye
So soft and kind;

His soul to Him, who gave it, rose;
God lead it to its long repose,
Its glorious rest!
And, though the warrior's sun has set,
Its light shall linger round us yet,
Bright, radiant, blest.

SONNETS

I
THE GOOD SHEPHERD

(EL BUEN PASTOR)
BY LOPE DE VEGA

Shepherd! who with thine amorous, sylvan song
   Hast broken the slumber that encompassed me,
   Who mad'st thy crook from the accursed tree,
   On which thy powerful arms were stretched so long!
Lead me to mercy's ever-flowing fountains;
   For thou my shepherd, guard, and guide shalt be;
   I will obey thy voice, and wait to see
   Thy feet all beautiful upon the mountains.
Hear, Shepherd! thou who for thy flock art dying,
   O, wash away these scarlet sins, for thou
   Rejoicest at the contrite sinner's vow.
O, wait! to thee my weary soul is crying,

Wait for me! Yet why ask it, when I see,
With feet nailed to the cross, thou 'rt waiting still for me!

II
TO-MORROW

(MANANA)
BY LOPE DE VEGA

Lord, what am I, that with unceasing care,
    Thou didst seek after me, that thou didst wait
    Wet with unhealthy dews, before my gate,
    And pass the gloomy nights of winter there?
O strange delusion! that I did not greet
    Thy blest approach, and O, to Heaven how lost,
    If my ingratitude's unkindly frost
    Has chilled the bleeding wounds upon thy feet.
How oft my guardian angel gently cried,
    "Soul, from thy casement look, and thou shalt see
    How he persists to knock and wait for thee!"
And, O! how often to that voice of sorrow,
    "To-morrow we will open," I replied,
    And when the morrow came I answered still "To-morrow."

III
THE NATIVE LAND

(EL PATRIO CIELO)
BY FRANCISCO DE ALDANA

Clear fount of light! my native land on high,
    Bright with a glory that shall never fade!
    Mansion of truth! without a veil or shade,
    Thy holy quiet meets the spirit's eye.
There dwells the soul in its ethereal essence,
    Gasping no longer for life's feeble breath;
    But, sentinelled in heaven, its glorious presence

With pitying eye beholds, yet fears not, death.
Beloved country! banished from thy shore,
    A stranger in this prison-house of clay,
    The exiled spirit weeps and sighs for thee!
Heavenward the bright perfections I adore
    Direct, and the sure promise cheers the way,
    That, whither love aspires, there shall my dwelling be.

IV
THE IMAGE OF GOD

(LA IMAGEN DE DIOS)
BY FRANCISCO DE ALDANA

O Lord! who seest, from yon starry height,
    Centred in one the future and the past,
    Fashioned in thine own image, see how fast
    The world obscures in me what once was bright!
Eternal Sun! the warmth which thou hast given,
    To cheer life's flowery April, fast decays;
    Yet in the hoary winter of my days,
    Forever green shall be my trust in Heaven.
Celestial King! O let thy presence pass
    Before my spirit, and an image fair
    Shall meet that look of mercy from on high,
As the reflected image in a glass
    Doth meet the look of him who seeks it there,
    And owes its being to the gazer's eye.

V
THE BROOK

(A UN ARROYUELO)
ANONYMOUS

Laugh of the mountain!—lyre of bird and tree!
    Pomp of the meadow! mirror of the morn!

The soul of April, unto whom are born
The rose and jessamine, leaps wild in thee!
Although, where'er thy devious current strays,
    The lap of earth with gold and silver teems,
    To me thy clear proceeding brighter seems
    Than golden sands, that charm each shepherd's gaze.
How without guile thy bosom, all transparent
    As the pure crystal, lets the curious eye
    Thy secrets scan, thy smooth, round pebbles count!
How, without malice murmuring, glides thy current!
    O sweet simplicity of days gone by!
    Thou shun'st the haunts of man, to dwell in limpid fount!

ANCIENT SPANISH BALLADS.

In the chapter with this title in Outre-Mer, besides Illustrations from Byron and Lockhart are the three following examples, contributed by Mr. Longfellow.

I

Rio Verde, Rio Verde!
    Many a corpse is bathed in thee,
Both of Moors and eke of Christians,
    Slain with swords most cruelly.

And thy pure and crystal waters
    Dappled are with crimson gore;
For between the Moors and Christians
    Long has been the fight and sore.

Dukes and Counts fell bleeding near thee,
    Lords of high renown were slain,
Perished many a brave hidalgo
    Of the noblemen of Spain.

"King Alfonso the Eighth, having exhausted his treasury in war, wishes to lay a tax of five farthings upon each of the Castillan hidalgos, in order to defray the expenses of a journey from Burgos to Cuenca. This proposition of the king was met with disdain by the noblemen who had been assembled on the occasion."

Don Nuno, Count of Lara,
    In anger and in pride,
Forgot all reverence for the king,
    And thus in wrath replied:

"Our noble ancestors," quoth he,
    "Ne'er such a tribute paid;
Nor shall the king receive of us
    What they have once gainsaid.

"The base-born soul who deems it just
    May here with thee remain;
But follow me, ye cavaliers,
    Ye noblemen of Spain."

Forth followed they the noble Count,
    They marched to Glera's plain;
Out of three thousand gallant knights
    Did only three remain.

They tied the tribute to their spears,
    They raised it in the air,
And they sent to tell their lord the king
    That his tax was ready there.

"He may send and take by force," said they,
    "This paltry sum of gold;
But the goodly gift of liberty
    Cannot be bought and sold."

"One of the finest of the historic ballads is that which describes Bernardo's march to Roncesvalles. He sallies forth 'with three thousand Leonese and more,' to protect the glory and freedom of his native land. From all sides, the peasantry of the land flock to the hero's standard."

The peasant leaves his plough afield,
    The reaper leaves his hook,
And from his hand the shepherd-boy.
    Lets fall the pastoral crook.

The young set up a shout of joy,
    The old forget their years,
The feeble man grows stout of heart.
    No more the craven fears.

All rush to Bernard's standard,
    And on liberty they call;
They cannot brook to wear the yoke,
    When threatened by the Gaul.

"Free were we born," 't is thus they cry
    "And willingly pay we
The duty that we owe our king
    By the divine decree.

"But God forbid that we obey
    The laws of foreign knaves,
Tarnish the glory of our sires,
    And make our children slaves.

"Our hearts have not so craven grown,
    So bloodless all our veins,
So vigorless our brawny arms,
    As to submit to chains.

"Has the audacious Frank, forsooth,
    Subdued these seas and lands?
Shall he a bloodless victory have?
No, not while we have hands.

"He shall learn that the gallant Leonese
    Can bravely fight and fall,
But that they know not how to yield;
    They are Castilians all.

"Was it for this the Roman power
    Of old was made to yield
Unto Numantia's valiant hosts
    On many a bloody field?

"Shall the bold lions that have bathed
    Their paws in Libyan gore,
Crouch basely to a feebler foe,
    And dare the strife no more?

"Let the false king sell town and tower,
    But not his vassals free;
For to subdue the free-born soul
    No royal power hath he!"

VIDA DE SAN MILLAN

BY GONZALO DE BERCEO

And when the kings were in the field,—their squadrons in array,—
With lance in rest they onward pressed to mingle in the fray;
But soon upon the Christians fell a terror of their foes,—
These were a numerous army,—a little handful those.

And while the Christian people stood in this uncertainty,
Upward to heaven they turned their eyes, and fixed their thoughts
    on high;
And there two figures they beheld, all beautiful and bright,
Even than the pure new-fallen snow their garments were more white.

They rode upon two horses more white than crystal sheen,
And arms they bore such as before no mortal man had seen;
The one, he held a crosier,—a pontiff's mitre wore;
The other held a crucifix,—such man ne'er saw before.

Their faces were angelical, celestial forms had they,—
And downward through the fields of air they urged their rapid way;
They looked upon the Moorish host with fierce and angry look,
And in their hands, with dire portent, their naked sabres shook.

The Christian host, beholding this, straightway take heart again;
They fall upon their bended knees, all resting on the plain,
And each one with his clenched fist to smite his breast begins,
And promises to God on high he will forsake his sins.

And when the heavenly knights drew near unto the battle-ground,
They dashed among the Moors and dealt unerring blows around;
Such deadly havoc there they made the foremost ranks along,
A panic terror spread unto the hindmost of the throng.

Together with these two good knights, the champions of the sky,
The Christians rallied and began to smite full sore and high;
The Moors raised up their voices and by the Koran swore
That in their lives such deadly fray they ne'er had seen before.

Down went the misbelievers,—fast sped the bloody fight,—
Some ghastly and dismembered lay, and some half dead with fright:
Full sorely they repented that to the field they came,
For they saw that from the battle they should retreat with shame.

Another thing befell them,—they dreamed not of such woes,—
The very arrows that the Moors shot front their twanging bows
Turned back against them in their flight and wounded them full sore,
And every blow they dealt the foe was paid in drops of gore.

* * * * *

Now he that bore the crosier, and the papal crown had on,
Was the glorified Apostle, the brother of Saint John;

And he that held the crucifix, and wore the monkish hood,
Was the holy San Millan of Cogolla's neighborhood.

SAN MIGUEL, THE CONVENT

(SAN MIGUEL DE LA TUMBA)
BY GONZALO DE BERCEO

San Miguel de la Tumba is a convent vast and wide;
The sea encircles it around, and groans on every side:
It is a wild and dangerous place, and many woes betide
The monks who in that burial-place in penitence abide.

Within those dark monastic walls, amid the ocean flood,
Of pious, fasting monks there dwelt a holy brotherhood;
To the Madonna's glory there an altar high was placed,
And a rich and costly image the sacred altar graced.

Exalted high upon a throne, the Virgin Mother smiled,
And, as the custom is, she held within her arms the Child;
The kings and wise men of the East were kneeling by her side;
Attended was she like a queen whom God had sanctified.

* * * * *

Descending low before her face a screen of feathers hung,—
A moscader, or fan for flies, 'tis called in vulgar tongue;
From the feathers of the peacock's wing 't was fashioned bright and
    fair,
And glistened like the heaven above when all its stars are there.

It chanced that, for the people's sins, fell the lightning's blasting
    stroke:
Forth from all four the sacred walls the flames consuming broke;
The sacred robes were all consumed, missal and holy book;
And hardly with their lives the monks their crumbling walls
    forsook.

* * * * *

But though the desolating flame raged fearfully and wild,
It did not reach the Virgin Queen, it did not reach the Child;
It did not reach the feathery screen before her face that shone,
Nor injure in a farthing's worth the image or the throne.

The image it did not consume, it did not burn the screen;
Even in the value of a hair they were not hurt, I ween;
Not even the smoke did reach them, nor injure more the shrine
Than the bishop hight Don Tello has been hurt by hand of mine.

* * * * *

SONG

She is a maid of artless grace,
Gentle in form, and fair of face,

Tell me, thou ancient mariner,
    That sailest on the sea,
If ship, or sail or evening star
    Be half so fair as she!

Tell me, thou gallant cavalier,
    Whose shining arms I see,
If steel, or sword, or battle-field
    Be half so fair as she!

Tell me, thou swain, that guard'st thy flock
    Beneath the shadowy tree,
If flock, or vale, or mountain-ridge
    Be half so fair as she!

SANTA TERESA'S BOOK-MARK

(LETRILLA QUE LLEVABA POR REGISTRO EN SU BREVIARIO)
BY SANTA TERESA DE AVILA

Let nothing disturb thee,
Nothing affright thee;
All things are passing;
God never changeth;
Patient endurance
Attaineth to all things;
Who God possesseth
In nothing is wanting;
Alone God sufficeth.

FROM THE CANCIONEROS

I
EYES SO TRISTFUL, EYES SO TRISTFUL

(OJOS TRISTES, OJOS TRISTES)
BY DIEGO DE SALDANA

Eyes so tristful, eyes so tristful,
Heart so full of care and cumber,
I was lapped in rest and slumber,
Ye have made me wakeful, wistful!

In this life of labor endless
Who shall comfort my distresses?
Querulous my soul and friendless
In its sorrow shuns caresses.
Ye have made me, ye have made me
Querulous of you, that care not,

Eyes so tristful, yet I dare not
Say to what ye have betrayed me.

II
SOME DAY, SOME DAY

(ALGUNA VEZ)
BY CRISTOBAL DE GASTILLOJO

Some day, some day
O troubled breast,
Shalt thou find rest.

If Love in thee
To grief give birth,
Six feet of earth
Can more than he;
There calm and free
And unoppressed
Shalt thou find rest.

The unattained
In life at last,
When life is passed,
Shall all be gained;
And no more pained,
No more distressed,
Shalt thou find rest.

III
COME, O DEATH, SO SILENT FLYING

(VEN, MUERTE TAN ESCONDIDA)
BY EL COMMENDADOR ESCRIVA

Come, O Death, so silent flying
That unheard thy coming be,
Lest the sweet delight of dying
Bring life back again to me.

For thy sure approach perceiving,
In my constancy and pain
I new life should win again,
Thinking that I am not living.
So to me, unconscious lying,
All unknown thy coming be,
Lest the sweet delight of dying
Bring life back again to me.
Unto him who finds thee hateful,
Death, thou art inhuman pain;
But to me, who dying gain,
Life is but a task ungrateful.
Come, then, with my wish complying,
All unheard thy coming be,
Lest the sweet delight of dying
Bring life back again to me.

IV
GLOVE OF BLACK IN WHITE HAND BARE

Glove of black in white hand bare,
And about her forehead pale
Wound a thin, transparent veil,
That doth not conceal her hair;
Sovereign attitude and air,
Cheek and neck alike displayed
With coquettish charms arrayed,
Laughing eyes and fugitive;—
This is killing men that live,
'T is not mourning for the dead.

FROM THE SWEDISH AND DANISH

PASSAGES FROM FRITHIOF'S SAGA

BY ESAIAS TEGNER

I
FRITHIOF'S HOMESTEAD

Three miles extended around the fields of the homestead, on three
    sides
Valleys and mountains and hills, but on the fourth side was the
    ocean.
Birch woods crowned the summits, but down the slope of the
    hillsides
Flourished the golden corn, and man-high was waving the rye-field.
Lakes, full many in number, their mirror held up for the mountains,
Held for the forests up, in whose depths the high-horned reindeers
Had their kingly walk, and drank of a hundred brooklets.
But in the valleys widely around, there fed on the greensward
Herds with shining hides and udders that longed for the milk-pail.
'Mid these scattered, now here and now there, were numberless
    flocks of
Sheep with fleeces white, as thou seest the white-looking stray clouds,
Flock-wise spread o'er the heavenly vault when it bloweth in
    springtime.
Coursers two times twelve, all mettlesome, fast fettered storm-winds,
Stamping stood in the line of stalls, and tugged at their fodder.
Knotted with red were their manes, and their hoofs all white with
    steel shoes.
Th' banquet-hall, a house by itself, was timbered of hard fir.
Not five hundred men (at ten times twelve to the hundred)
Filled up the roomy hall, when assembled for drinking, at Yule-tide.
Through the hall, as long as it was, went a table of holm-oak,
Polished and white, as of steel; the columns twain of the High-seat
Stood at the end thereof, two gods carved out of an elm-tree:
Odin with lordly look, and Frey with the sun on his frontlet.

Lately between the two, on a bear-skin (the skin it was coal-black,
Scarlet-red was the throat, but the paws were shodden with silver),
Thorsten sat with his friends, Hospitality sitting with Gladness.
Oft, when the moon through the cloudrack flew, related the old man
Wonders from distant lands he had seen, and cruises of Vikings
Far away on the Baltic, and Sea of the West and the White Sea.
Hushed sat the listening bench, and their glances hung on the
    graybeard's
Lips, as a bee on the rose; but the Scald was thinking of Brage,
Where, with his silver beard, and runes on his tongue, he is seated
Under the leafy beech, and tells a tradition by Mimer's
Ever-murmuring wave, himself a living tradition.
Midway the floor (with thatch was it strewn) burned ever the fire-
    flame
Glad on its stone-built hearth; and thorough the wide-mouthed
    smoke-flue
Looked the stars, those heavenly friends, down into the great hall.
Round the walls, upon nails of steel, were hanging in order
Breastplate and helmet together, and here and there among them
Downward lightened a sword, as in winter evening a star shoots.
More than helmets and swords the shields in the hall were
    resplendent,
White as the orb of the sun, or white as the moon's disk of silver.
Ever and anon went a maid round the hoard, and filled up the drink-
    horns,
Ever she cast down her eyes and blushed; in the shield her reflection
Blushed, too, even as she; this gladdened the drinking champions.

II
A SLEDGE-RIDE ON THE ICE

King Ring with his queen to the banquet did fare,
On the lake stood the ice so mirror-clear,

"Fare not o'er the ice," the stranger cries;
"It will burst, and full deep the cold bath lies."

"The king drowns not easily," Ring outspake;
"He who's afraid may go round the lake."

Threatening and dark looked the stranger round,
His steel shoes with haste on his feet he bound,

The sledge-horse starts forth strong and free;
He snorteth flames, so glad is he.

"Strike out," screamed the king, "my trotter good,
Let us see if thou art of Sleipner's blood."

They go as a storm goes over the lake.
No heed to his queen doth the old man take.

But the steel-shod champion standeth not still,
He passeth them by as swift as he will.

He carves many runes in the frozen tide,
Fair Ingeborg o'er her own name doth glide.

III
FRITHIOF'S TEMPTATION

Spring is coming, birds are twittering, forests leaf, and smiles the sun,
And the loosened torrents downward, singing, to the ocean run;
Glowing like the cheek of Freya, peeping rosebuds 'gin to ope,
And in human hearts awaken love of life, and joy, and hope.

Now will hunt the ancient monarch, and the queen shall join the
    sport:
Swarming in its gorgeous splendor, is assembled all the Court;
Bows ring loud, and quivers rattle, stallions paw the ground alway,
And, with hoods upon their eyelids, scream the falcons for their prey.

See, the Queen of the Chase advances! Frithiof, gaze not at the sight!
Like a star upon a spring-cloud sits she on her palfrey white.
Half of Freya, half of Rota, yet more beauteous than these two,
And from her light hat of purple wave aloft the feathers blue.

Gaze not at her eyes' blue heaven, gaze not at her golden hair!
Oh beware! her waist is slender, full her bosom is, beware!

Look not at the rose and lily on her cheek that shifting play,
List not to the voice beloved, whispering like the wind of May.

Now the huntsman's band is ready. Hurrah! over hill and dale!
Horns ring, and the hawks right upward to the hall of Odin sail.
All the dwellers in the forest seek in fear their cavern homes,
But, with spear outstretched before her, after them the Valkyr comes.

* * * * *

Then threw Frithiof down his mantle, and upon the greensward
    spread,
And the ancient king so trustful laid on Frithiof's knee his head,
Slept as calmly as the hero sleepeth, after war's alarm,
On his shield, or as an infant sleeps upon its mother's arm.

As he slumbers, hark! there sings a coal-black bird upon the bough;
"Hasten, Frithiof, slay the old man, end your quarrel at a blow:
Take his queen, for she is thine, and once the bridal kiss she gave,
Now no human eye beholds thee, deep and silent is the grave,"

Frithiof listens; hark! there sings a snow-white bird upon the bough:
"Though no human eye beholds thee, Odin's eye beholds thee now.
Coward! wilt thou murder sleep, and a defenceless old man slay!
Whatsoe'er thou winn'st, thou canst not win a hero's fame this way."

Thus the two wood-birds did warble: Frithiof took his war-sword
    good,
With a shudder hurled it from him, far into the gloomy wood.
Coal-black bird flies down to Nastrand, but on light, unfolded wings,
Like the tone of harps, the other, sounding towards the sun,
    upsprings.

Straight the ancient king awakens. "Sweet has been my sleep," he said;
"Pleasantly sleeps one in the shadow, guarded by a brave man's blade.
But where is thy sword, O stranger? Lightning's brother, where is he?
Who thus parts you, who should never from each other parted be?"

"It avails not," Frithiof answered; "in the North are other swords:

Sharp, O monarch! is the sword's tongue, and it speaks not peaceful
    words;
Murky spirits dwell in steel blades, spirits from the Niffelhem;
Slumber is not safe before them, silver locks but anger them."

IV
FRITHIOF'S FAREWELL

No more shall I see
In its upward motion
The smoke of the Northland. Man is a slave:
The fates decree.
On the waste of the ocean
There is my fatherland, there is my grave.

Go not to the strand,
Ring, with thy bride,
After the stars spread their light through the sky.
Perhaps in the sand,
Washed up by the tide,
The bones of the outlawed Viking may lie.

Then, quoth the king,
"'T is mournful to hear
A man like a whimpering maiden cry.
The death-song they sing
Even now in mine ear,
What avails it? He who is born must die."

* * * * *

THE CHILDREN OF THE LORD'S SUPPER

BY ESAIAS TEGNER

Pentecost, day of rejoicing, had come. The church of the village
Gleaming stood in the morning's sheen.
        On the spire of the bell

Decked with a brazen cock, the friendly flames of the Spring-sun
Glanced like the tongues of fire, beheld by Apostles aforetime.
Clear was the heaven and blue, and May, with her cap crowned with
    roses,
Stood in her holiday dress in the fields, and the wind and the brooklet
Murmured gladness and peace, God's-peace! with lips rosy-tinted
Whispered the race of the flowers, and merry on balancing branches
Birds were singing their carol, a jubilant hymn to the Highest.
Swept and clean was the churchyard. Adorned like a leaf-woven arbor
Stood its old-fashioned gate; and within upon each cross of iron
Hung was a fragrant garland, new twined by the hands of affection.
Even the dial, that stood on a mound among the departed,
(There full a hundred years had it stood,) was embellished with
    blossoms
Like to the patriarch hoary, the sage of his kith and the hamlet,
Who on his birthday is crowned by children and children's children,
So stood the ancient prophet, and mute with his pencil of iron
Marked on the tablet of stone, and measured the time and its
    changes,
While all around at his feet, an eternity slumbered in quiet.
Also the church within was adorned, for this was the season
When the young, their parents' hope, and the loved-ones of heaven,
Should at the foot of the altar renew the vows of their baptism.
Therefore each nook and corner was swept and cleaned, and the dust
    was
Blown from the walls and ceiling, and from the oil-painted benches.
There stood the church like a garden; the Feast of the Leafy Pavilions
Saw we in living presentment. From noble arms on the church wall
Grew forth a cluster of leaves, and the preacher's pulpit of oak-wood
Budded once more anew, as aforetime the rod before Aaron.
Wreathed thereon was the Bible with leaves, and the dove, washed
    with silver
Under its canopy fastened, had on it a necklace of wind-flowers.
But in front of the choir, round the altar-piece painted by Horberg,
Crept a garland gigantic; and bright-curling tresses of angels
Peeped, like the sun from a cloud, from out of the shadowy leaf-
    work.
Likewise the lustre of brass, new-polished, blinked from the ceiling,
And for lights there were lilies of Pentecost set in the sockets.

Loud rang the bells already; the thronging crowd was assembled
Far from valleys and hills, to list to the holy preaching.
Hark! then roll forth at once the mighty tones of the organ,
Hover like voices from God, aloft like invisible spirits.
Like as Elias in heaven, when he cast from off him his mantle,
So cast off the soul its garments of earth; and with one voice
Chimed in the congregation, and sang an anthem immortal
Of the sublime Wallin, of David's harp in the North-land
Tuned to the choral of Luther; the song on its mighty pinions
Took every living soul, and lifted it gently to heaven,
And each face did shine like the Holy One's face upon Tabor.
Lo! there entered then into the church the Reverend Teacher.
Father he hight and he was in the parish; a Christianly plainness
Clothed from his head to his feet the old man of seventy winters.
Friendly was he to behold, and glad as the heralding angel
Walked he among the crowds, but still a contemplative grandeur
Lay on his forehead as clear as on moss-covered gravestone a sunbeam.
As in his inspiration (an evening twilight that faintly
Gleams in the human soul, even now, from the day of creation)
Th' Artist, the friend of heaven, imagines Saint John when in Patmos,
Gray, with his eyes uplifted to heaven, so seemed then the old man:
Such was the glance of his eye, and such were his tresses of silver.
All the congregation arose in the pews that were numbered.
But with a cordial look, to the right and the left hand, the old man
Nodding all hail and peace, disappeared in the innermost chancel.

Simply and solemnly now proceeded the Christian service,
Singing and prayer, and at last an ardent discourse from the old man.
Many a moving word and warning, that out of the heart came,
Fell like the dew of the morning, like manna on those in the desert.
Then, when all was finished, the Teacher re-entered the chancel
Followed therein by the young. The boys on the right had their places,
Delicate figures, with close-curling hair and cheeks rosy-blooming.
But on the left of these there stood the tremulous lilies,
Tinged with the blushing light of the dawn, the diffident maidens,—
Folding their hands in prayer, and their eyes cast down on the pavement

Now came, with question and answer, the catechism. In the beginning
Answered the children with troubled and faltering voice, but the old
man's
Glances of kindness encouraged them soon, and the doctrines
eternal
Flowed, like the waters of fountains, so clear from lips unpolluted.
Each time the answer was closed, and as oft as they named the
Redeemer,
Lowly louted the boys, and lowly the maidens all courtesied.
Friendly the Teacher stood, like an angel of light there among them.
And to the children explained the holy, the highest, in few words,
Thorough, yet simple and clear, for sublimity always is simple,
Both in sermon and song, a child can seize on its meaning.
E'en as the green-growing bud unfolds when Springtide approaches.
Leaf by leaf puts forth, and warmed, by the radiant sunshine,
Blushes with purple and gold, till at last the perfected blossom
Opens its odorous chalice, and rocks with its crown in the breezes,
So was unfolded here the Christian lore of salvation,
Line by line from the soul of childhood. The fathers and mothers
Stood behind them in tears, and were glad at the well-worded answer.

Now went the old man up to the altar;—and straightway
transfigured
(So did it seem unto me) was then the affectionate Teacher.
Like the Lord's Prophet sublime, and awful as Death and as
Judgment
Stood he, the God-commissioned, the soul-searcher, earthward
descending
Glances, sharp as a sword, into hearts that to him were transparent
Shot he; his voice was deep, was low like the thunder afar off.
So on a sudden transfigured he stood there, lie spake and he
questioned.

"This is the faith of the Fathers, the faith the Apostles
delivered,
This is moreover the faith whereunto I baptized you, while still ye
Lay on your mothers' breasts, and nearer the portals of heaven,
Slumbering received you then the Holy Church in its bosom;
Wakened from sleep are ye now, and the light in its radiant splendor

Downward rains from the heaven;—to-day on the threshold of childhood
Kindly she frees you again, to examine and make your election,
For she knows naught of compulsion, and only conviction desireth.
This is the hour of your trial, the turning-point of existence,
Seed for the coming days; without revocation departeth
Now from your lips the confession; Bethink ye, before ye make answer!
Think not, O think not with guile to deceive the questioning Teacher.
Sharp is his eye to-day, and a curse ever rests upon falsehood.
Enter not with a lie on Life's journey; the multitude hears you,
Brothers and sisters and parents, what dear upon earth is and holy
Standeth before your sight as a witness; the Judge everlasting
Looks from the sun down upon you, and angels in waiting beside him
Grave your confession in letters of fire upon tablets eternal.
Thus, then,—believe ye in God, in the Father who this world created?
Him who redeemed it, the Son, and the Spirit where both are united?
Will ye promise me here, (a holy promise!) to cherish
God more than all things earthly, and every man as a brother?
Will ye promise me here, to confirm your faith by your living,
Th' heavenly faith of affection! to hope, to forgive, and to suffer,
Be what it may your condition, and walk before God in uprightness?
Will ye promise me this before God and man?"—With a clear voice
Answered the young men Yes! and Yes! with lips softly-breathing
Answered the maidens eke. Then dissolved from the brow of the Teacher
Clouds with the lightnings therein, and lie spake in accents more gentle,
Soft as the evening's breath, as harps by Babylon's rivers.

       "Hail, then, hail to you all! To the heirdom of heaven be ye welcome!
Children no more from this day, but by covenant brothers and sisters!
Yet,—for what reason not children? Of such is the kingdom of heaven.
Here upon earth an assemblage of children, in heaven one Father,
Ruling them all as his household,—forgiving in turn and chastising,
That is of human life a picture, as Scripture has taught us.
Blest are the pure before God! Upon purity and upon virtue

Resteth the Christian Faith: she herself from on high is descended.
Strong as a man and pure as a child, is the sum of the doctrine,
Which the Divine One taught, and suffered and died on the cross for
Oh, as ye wander this day from childhood's sacred asylum
Downward and ever downward, and deeper in Age's chill valley,
Oh, how soon will ye come,—too soon!—and long to turn backward
Up to its hill-tops again, to the sun-illumined, where Judgment
Stood like a father before you, and Pardon, clad like a mother,
Gave you her hand to kiss, and the loving heart was for given
Life was a play and your hands grasped after the roses of heaven!
Seventy years have I lived already; the Father eternal
Gave rue gladness and care; but the loveliest hours of existence,
When I have steadfastly gazed in their eyes, I have instantly known
    them,
Known them all again;—the were my childhood's acquaintance.
Therefore take from henceforth, as guides in the paths of existence,
Prayer, with her eyes raised to heaven, and Innocence, bride of man's
    childhood
Innocence, child beloved, is a guest from the world of the blessed,
Beautiful, and in her hand a lily; on life's roaring billows
Swings she in safety, she heedeth them not in the ship she is sleeping.
Calmly she gazes around in the turmoil of men; in the desert
Angels descend and minister unto her; she herself knoweth
Naught of her glorious attendance; but follows faithful and humble,
Follows so long as she may her friend; oh do not reject her,
For she cometh from God and she holdeth the keys of the heavens.
Prayer is Innocence' friend; and willingly flieth incessant
'Twixt the earth and the sky, the carrier-pigeon of heaven,
Son of Eternity, fettered in Time, and an exile, the Spirit
Tugs at his chains evermore, and struggles like flame ever upward.
Still he recalls with emotion his Father's manifold mansions,
Thinks of the land of his fathers, where blossomed more freshly the
    flowerets,
Shone a more beautiful sun, and he played with the winged angels.
Then grows the earth too narrow, too close; and homesick for heaven
Longs the wanderer again; and the Spirit's longings are worship;
Worship is called his most beautiful hour, and its tongue is entreaty.
Aid when the infinite burden of life descendeth upon us,
Crushes to earth our hope, and, under the earth, in the graveyard,

Then it is good to pray unto God; for his sorrowiug children
Turns he ne'er from his door, but he heals and helps and consoles
     them,
Yet is it better to pray when all things are prosperous with us,
Pray in fortunate days, for life's most beautiful Fortune
Kneels before the Eternal's throne; and with hands interfolded,
Praises thankful and moved the only giver of blessings.
Or do ye know, ye children, one blessing that comes not from
     Heaven?
What has mankind forsooth, the poor! that it has not received?
Therefore, fall in the dust and pray! The seraphs adoring
Cover with pinions six their face in the glory of him who
Hung his masonry pendent on naught, when the world be created.
Earth declareth his might, and the firmament utters his glory.
Races blossom and die, and stars fall downward from heaven,
Downward like withered leaves; at the last stroke of midnight,
     millenniums
Lay themselves down at his feet, and he sees them, but counts them
     as nothing
Who shall stand in his presence? The wrath of the judge is terrific,
Casting the insolent down at a glance. When he speaks in his anger
Hillocks skip like the kid, and mountains leap like the roebuck.
Yet,—why are ye afraid, ye children? This awful avenger,
Ah! is a merciful God! God's voice was not in the earthquake,
Not in the fire, nor the storm, but it was in the whispering breezes.
Love is the root of creation; God's essence; worlds without number
Lie in his bosom like children; he made them for this purpose only.
Only to love and to be loved again, he breathed forth his spirit
Into the slumbering dust, and upright standing, it laid its
Hand on its heart, and felt it was warm with a flame out of heaven.
Quench, oh quench not that flame! It is the breath of your being.
Love is life, but hatred is death. Not father, nor mother
Loved you, as God has loved you; for 't was that you may be happy
Gave he his only Son. When he bowed down his head in the death-
     hour
Solemnized Love its triumph; the sacrifice then was completed.
Lo! then was rent on a sudden the veil of the temple, dividing
Earth and heaven apart, and the dead from their sepulchres rising
Whispered with pallid lips and low in the ears of each other

Th' answer, but dreamed of before, to creation's enigma,—
  Atonement!
Depths of Love are Atonement's depths, for Love is Atonement.
Therefore, child of mortality, love thou the merciful Father;
Wish what the Holy One wishes, and not from fear, but affection
Fear is the virtue of slaves; but the heart that loveth is willing
Perfect was before God, and perfect is Love, and Love only.
Lovest thou God as thou oughtest, then lovest thou likewise thy
  brethren:
One is the sun in heaven, and one, only one, is Love also.
Bears not each human figure the godlike stamp on his forehead
Readest thou not in his face thou origin? Is he not sailing
Lost like thyself on an ocean unknown, and is he not guided
By the same stars that guide thee? Why shouldst thou hate then thy
  brother?
Hateth he thee, forgive! For 't is sweet to stammer one letter
Of the Eternal's language;—on earth it is called Forgiveness!
Knowest thou Him, who forgave, with the crown of thorns on his
  temples?
Earnestly prayed for his foes, for his murderers? Say, dost thou know
  him?
Ah! thou confessest his name, so follow likewise his example,
Think of thy brother no ill, but throw a veil over his failings,
Guide the erring aright; for the good, the heavenly shepherd
Took the lost lamb in his arms, and bore it back to its mother.
This is the fruit of Love, and it is by its fruits that we know it.
Love is the creature's welfare, with God; but Love among mortals
Is but an endless sigh! He longs, and endures, and stands waiting,
Suffers and yet rejoices, and smiles with tears on his eyelids.
Hope,—so is called upon earth, his recompense, Hope, the
  befriending,
Does what she can, for she points evermore up to heaven, and
  faithful
Plunges her anchor's peak in the depths of the grave, and beneath it
Paints a more beautiful world, a dim, but a sweet play of shadows!
Races, better than we, have leaned on her wavering promise,
Having naught else but Hope. Then praise we our Father in heaven,
Him, who has given us more; for to us has Hope been transfigured,
Groping no longer in night; she is Faith, she is living assurance.

Faith is enlightened Hope; she is light, is the eye of affection,
Dreams of the longing interprets, and carves their visions in marble.
Faith is the sun of life; and her countenance shines like the Hebrew's,
For she has looked upon God; the heaven on its stable foundation
Draws she with chains down to earth, and the New Jerusalem sinketh
Splendid with portals twelve in golden vapors descending.
There enraptured she wanders. and looks at the figures majestic,
Fears not the winged crowd, in the midst of them all is her
    homestead.
Therefore love and believe; for works will follow spontaneous
Even as day does the sun; the Right from the Good is an offspring,
Love in a bodily shape; and Christian works are no more than
Animate Love and faith, as flowers are the animate Springtide.
Works do follow us all unto God; there stand and bear witness
Not what they seemed,—but what they were only. Blessed is he who
Hears their confession secure; they are mute upon earth until death's
    hand
Opens the mouth of the silent. Ye children, does Death e'er alarm
    you?
Death is the brother of Love, twin-brother is he, and is only
More austere to behold. With a kiss upon lips that are fading
Takes he the soul and departs, and, rocked in the arms of affection,
Places the ransomed child, new born, 'fore the face of its father.
Sounds of his coming already I hear,—see dimly his pinions,
Swart as the night, but with stars strewn upon them! I fear not before
    him.
Death is only release, and in mercy is mute. On his bosom
Freer breathes, in its coolness, my breast; and face to face standing
Look I on God as he is, a sun unpolluted by vapors;
Look on the light of the ages I loved, the spirits majestic,
Nobler, better than I; they stand by the throne all transfigured,
Vested in white, and with harps of gold, and are singing an anthem,
Writ in the climate of heaven, in the language spoken by angels.
You, in like manner, ye children beloved, he one day shall gather,
Never forgets he the weary;—then welcome, ye loved ones, hereafter!
Meanwhile forget not the keeping of vows, forget not the promise,
Wander from holiness onward to holiness; earth shall ye heed not
Earth is but dust and heaven is light; I have pledged you to heaven.
God of the universe, hear me! thou fountain of Love everlasting,

Hark to the voice of thy servant! I send up my prayer to thy heaven!
Let me hereafter not miss at thy throne one spirit of all these,
Whom thou hast given me here! I have loved them all like a father.
May they bear witness for me, that I taught them the way of salvation,
Faithful, so far as I knew, of thy word; again may they know me,
Fall on their Teacher's breast, and before thy face may I place them,
Pure as they now are, but only more tried, and exclaiming with gladness,
Father, lo! I am here, and the children, whom thou hast given me!"

   Weeping he spake in these words; and now at the beck of the old man
Knee against knee they knitted a wreath round the altar's enclosure.
Kneeling he read then the prayers of the consecration, and softly
With him the children read; at the close, with tremulous accents,
Asked he the peace of Heaven, a benediction upon them.
Now should have ended his task for the day; the following Sunday
Was for the young appointed to eat of the Lord's holy Supper.
Sudden, as struck from the clouds, stood the Teacher silent and laid his
Hand on his forehead, and cast his looks upward; while thoughts high and holy,
Flew through the midst of his soul, and his eyes glanced with wonderful brightness.
"On the next Sunday, who knows! perhaps I shall rest in the graveyard!
Some one perhaps of yourselves, a lily broken untimely,
Bow down his head to the earth; why delay I? the hour is accomplished,
Warm is the heart;—I will! for to-day grows the harvest of heaven.
What I began accomplish I now; what failing therein is
I, the old man, will answer to God and the reverend father.
Say to me only, ye children, ye denizens new-come in heaven,
Are ye ready this day to eat of the bread of Atonement?
What it denoteth, that know ye full well, I have told it you often.
Of the new covenant symbol it is, of Atonement a token,
Stablished between earth and heaven. Man by his sins and transgressions

Far has wandered from God, from his essence. 'T was in the
  beginning
Fast by the Tree of Knowledge he fell, and it hangs its crown o'er the
Fall to this day; in the Thought is the Fall; in the Heart the
  Atonement.
Infinite is the fall,—the Atonement infinite likewise.
See! behind me, as far as the old man remembers, and forward,
Far as Hope in her flight can reach with her wearied pinions,
Sin and Atonement incessant go through the lifetime of mortals.
Sin is brought forth full-grown; but Atonement sleeps in our bosoms
Still as the cradled babe; and dreams of heaven and of angels,
Cannot awake to sensation; is like the tones in the harp's strings,
Spirits imprisoned, that wait evermore the deliverer's finger.
Therefore, ye children beloved, descended the Prince of Atonement,
Woke the slumberer from sleep, and she stands now with eyes all
  resplendent.
Bright as the vault of the sky, and battles with Sin and o'ercomes her.
Downward to earth he came and, transfigured, thence reascended,
Not from the heart in like wise, for there he still lives in the Spirit,
Loves and atones evermore. So long as Time is, is Atonement.
Therefore with reverence take this day her visible token.
Tokens are dead if the things live not. The light everlasting
Unto the blind is not, but is born of the eye that has vision.
Neither in bread nor in wine, but in the heart that is hallowed
Lieth forgiveness enshrined; the intention alone of amendment
Fruits of the earth ennobles to heavenly things, and removes all
Sin and the guerdon of sin. Only Love with his arms wide extended,
Penitence wee ping and praying; the Will that is tried, and whose gold
  flows
Purified forth from the flames; in a word, mankind by Atonement
Breaketh Atonement's bread, and drinketh Atonement's wine-cup.
But he who cometh up hither, unworthy, with hate in his bosom,
Scoffing at men and at God, is guilty of Christ's blessed body,
And the Redeemer's blood! To himself he eateth and drinketh
Death and doom! And from this, preserve us, thou heavenly Father!
Are ye ready, ye children, to eat of the bread of Atonement?"
Thus with emotion he asked, and together answered the children,
"Yes!" with deep sobs interrupted. Then read he the due
  supplications,

Read the Form of Communion, and in chimed the organ and
anthem:
"O Holy Lamb of God, who takest away our transgressions,
Hear us! give us thy peace! have mercy, have mercy upon us!"
Th' old man, with trembling hand, and heavenly pearls on his eyelids,
Filled now the chalice and paten, and dealt round the mystical
symbols.
Oh, then seemed it to me as if God, with the broad eye of midday,
Clearer looked in at the windows, and all the trees in the church
yard
Bowed down their summits of green, and the grass on the graves
'gan to shiver
But in the children (I noted it well; I knew it) there ran a
Tremor of holy rapture along through their ice-cold members.
Decked like an altar before them, there stood the green earth, and
above it
Heaven opened itself, as of old before Stephen; they saw there
Radiant in glory the Father, and on his right hand the Redeemer.
Under them hear they the clang of harpstrings, and angels from gold
clouds
Beckon to them like brothers, and fan with their pinions of purple.

Closed was the Teacher's task, and with heaven in their hearts
and their faces,
Up rose the children all, and each bowed him, weeping full sorely,
Downward to kiss that reverend hand, but all of them pressed he
Moved to his bosom, and laid, with a prayer, his hands full of
blessings,
Now on the holy breast, and now on the innocent tresses.

* * * * *

KING CHRISTIAN

A NATIONAL SONG OF DENMARK

King Christian stood by the lofty mast
In mist and smoke;

His sword was hammering so fast,
Through Gothic helm and brain it passed;
Then sank each hostile hulk and mast,
        In mist and smoke.
"Fly!" shouted they, "fly, he who can!
Who braves of Denmark's Christian
        The stroke?"

Nils Juel gave heed to the tempest's roar,
        Now is the hour!
He hoisted his blood-red flag once more,
And smote upon the foe full sore,
And shouted Loud, through the tempest's roar,
        "Now is the hour!"
"Fly!" shouted they, "for shelter fly!
Of Denmark's Juel who can defy
        The power?"

North Sea! a glimpse of Wessel rent
        Thy murky sky!
Then champions to thine arms were sent;
Terror and Death glared where he went;
From the waves was heard a wail, that
        rent
        Thy murky sky!
From Denmark, thunders Tordenskiol',
Let each to Heaven commend his soul,
        And fly!

Path of the Dane to fame and might!
        Dark-rolling wave!
Receive thy friend, who, scorning flight
Goes to meet danger with despite,
Proudly as thou the tempest's might
        Dark-rolling wave!
And amid pleasures and alarm;
And war and victory, be thine arms
        My grave!

THE ELECTED KNIGHT

Sir Oluf he rideth over the plain,
    Full seven miles broad and seven miles wide,
But never, ah never can meet with the man
    A tilt with him dare ride.

He saw under the hillside
    A Knight full well equipped;
His steed was black, his helm was barred;
    He was riding at full speed.

He wore upon his spurs
    Twelve little golden birds;
Anon he spurred his steed with a clang,
    And there sat all the birds and sang.

He wore upon his mail
    Twelve little golden wheels;
Anon in eddies the wild wind blew,
    And round and round the wheels they flew.

He wore before his breast
    A lance that was poised in rest;
And it was sharper than diamond-stone,
    It made Sir Oluf's heart to groan.

He wore upon his helm
    A wreath of ruddy gold;
And that gave him the Maidens Three,
    The youngest was fair to behold.

Sir Oluf questioned the Knight eftsoon
    If he were come from heaven down;
"Art thou Christ of Heaven," quoth he,
    "So will I yield me unto thee."

"I am not Christ the Great,
    Thou shalt not yield thee yet;

I am an Unknown Knight,
   Three modest Maidens have me bedight."

"Art thou a Knight elected,
   And have three Maidens thee bedight
So shalt thou ride a tilt this day,
   For all the Maidens' honor!"

The first tilt they together rode
   They put their steeds to the test,
The second tilt they together rode,
   They proved their manhood best.

The third tilt they together rode,
   Neither of them would yield;
The fourth tilt they together rode,
   They both fell on the field.

Now lie the lords upon the plain,
   And their blood runs unto death;
Now sit the Maidens in the high tower,
   The youngest sorrows till death.

CHILDHOOD

BY JENS IMMANUEL BAGGESEN

There was a time when I was very small,
   When my whole frame was but an ell in height;
Sweetly, as I recall it, tears do fall,
   And therefore I recall it with delight.

I sported in my tender mother's arms,
   And rode a-horseback on best father's knee;
Alike were sorrows, passions and alarms,
   And gold, and Greek, and love, unknown to me,

Then seemed to me this world far less in size,
   Likewise it seemed to me less wicked far;

Like points in heaven, I saw the stars arise,
    And longed for wings that I might catch a star.

I saw the moon behind the island fade,
    And thought, "Oh, were I on that island there,
I could find out of what the moon is made,
    Find out how large it is, how round, how fair!"

Wondering, I saw God's sun, through western skies,
    Sink in the ocean's golden lap at night,
And yet upon the morrow early rise,
    And paint the eastern heaven with crimson light;

And thought of God, the gracious Heavenly Father,
    Who made me, and that lovely sun on high,
And all those pearls of heaven thick-strung together,
    Dropped, clustering, from his hand o'er all the sky.

With childish reverence, my young lips did say
    The prayer my pious mother taught to me:
"O gentle God! oh, let me strive alway
    Still to be wise, and good, and follow Thee!"

So prayed I for my father and my mother,
    And for my sister, and for all the town;
The king I knew not, and the beggar-brother,
    Who, bent with age, went, sighing, up and down.

They perished, the blithe days of boyhood perished,
    And all the gladness, all the peace I knew!
Now have I but their memory, fondly cherished;—
    God! may I never lose that too!

FROM THE GERMAN

THE HAPPIEST LAND

There sat one day in quiet,
   By an alehouse on the Rhine,
Four hale and hearty fellows,
   And drank the precious wine.

The landlord's daughter filled their cups,
   Around the rustic board
Then sat they all so calm and still,
   And spake not one rude word.

But, when the maid departed,
   A Swabian raised his hand,
And cried, all hot and flushed with wine,
   "Long live the Swabian land!

"The greatest kingdom upon earth
   Cannot with that compare
With all the stout and hardy men
   And the nut-brown maidens there.

"Ha!" cried a Saxon, laughing,
   And dashed his heard with wine;
"I had rather live in Laplaud,
   Than that Swabian land of thine!

"The goodliest land on all this earth,
   It is the Saxon land
There have I as many maidens
   As fingers on this hand!"

"Hold your tongues! both Swabian
         and Saxon!"
   A bold Bohemian cries;

"If there's a heaven upon this earth,
    In Bohemia it lies.

"There the tailor blows the flute,
    And the cobbler blows the horn,
And the miner blows the bugle,
    Over mountain gorge and bourn."

* * * * *

And then the landlord's daughter
Up to heaven raised her hand,
And said, "Ye may no more contend,—
There lies the happiest land!"

THE WAVE

BY CHRISTOPH AUGUST TIEDGE

"Whither, thou turbid wave?
Whither, with so much haste,
As if a thief wert thou?"

"I am the Wave of Life,
Stained with my margin's dust;
From the struggle and the strife
Of the narrow stream I fly
To the Sea's immensity,
To wash from me the slime
Of the muddy banks of Time."

THE DEAD

BY ERNST STOCKMANN

How they so softly rest,
All they the holy ones,
Unto whose dwelling-place
Now doth my soul draw near!
How they so softly rest,

All in their silent graves,
Deep to corruption
Slowly don-sinking!

And they no longer weep,
Here, where complaint is still!
And they no longer feel,
Here, where all gladness flies!
And, by the cypresses
Softly o'ershadowed
Until the Angel
Calls them, they slumber!

THE BIRD AND THE SHIP

BY WILHELM MULLER

"The rivers rush into the sea,
  By castle and town they go;
The winds behind them merrily
  Their noisy trumpets blow.

"The clouds are passing far and high,
  We little birds in them play;
And everything, that can sing and fly,
  Goes with us, and far away.

"I greet thee, bonny boat! Whither,
              or whence,
  With thy fluttering golden band?"—
"I greet thee, little bird! To the wide sea
  I haste from the narrow land.

"Full and swollen is every sail;
  I see no longer a hill,
I have trusted all to the sounding gale,
  And it will not let me stand still.

"And wilt thou, little bird, go with us?
　　Thou mayest stand on the mainmast tall,
For full to sinking is my house
　　With merry companions all."—

"I need not and seek not company,
　　Bonny boat, I can sing all alone;
For the mainmast tall too heavy am I,
　　Bonny boat, I have wings of my own.

"High over the sails, high over the mast,
　　Who shall gainsay these joys?
When thy merry companions are still, at last,
　　Thou shalt hear the sound of my voice.

"Who neither may rest, nor listen may,
　　God bless them every one!
I dart away, in the bright blue day,
　　And the golden fields of the sun.

"Thus do I sing my merry song,
　　Wherever the four winds blow;
And this same song, my whole life long,
　　Neither Poet nor Printer may know.'

WHITHER?

BY WILHELM MULLER

I heard a brooklet gushing
　　From its rocky fountain near,
Down into the valley rushing,
　　So fresh and wondrous clear.

I　know not what came o'er me,
　　Nor who the counsel gave;
But I must hasten downward,
　　All with my pilgrim-stave;

Downward, and ever farther,
        And ever the brook beside;
And ever fresher murmured,
And ever clearer, the tide.

Is this the way I was going?
Whither, O brooklet, say I
Thou hast, with thy soft murmur,
Murmured my senses away.

What do I say of a murmur?
That can no murmur be;
'T is the water-nymphs, that are singing
Their roundelays under me.

Let them sing, my friend, let them murmur,
    And wander merrily near;
The wheels of a mill are going
In every brooklet clear.

BEWARE!

(HUT DU DICH!)

I know a maiden fair to see,
        Take care!
She   can both false and friendly be,
        Beware! Beware!
        Trust her not,
She is fooling thee!

She   has two eyes, so soft and brown,
        Take care!
She   gives a side-glance and looks down,
        Beware! Beware!
        Trust her not,
She is fooling thee!

And she has hair of a golden hue,
　　Take care!
And　what she says, it is not true,
　　Beware! Beware!
　　Trust her not,
She is fooling thee!

She　has a bosom as white as snow,
　　Take care!
She knows how much it is best to show,
　　Beware! Beware!
　　Trust her not,
She is fooling thee!

She　gives thee a garland woven fair,
　　Take care!
It is a fool's-cap for thee to wear,
　　Beware! Beware!
　　Trust her not,
She is fooling thee!

SONG OF THE BELL

Bell! thou soundest merrily,
When the bridal party
　To the church doth hie!
Bell! thou soundest solemnly.
When, on Sabbath morning,
　Fields deserted lie!

Bell! thou soundest merrily;
Tellest thou at evening,
　Bed-time draweth nigh!
Bell! thou soundest mournfully.
Tellest thou the bitter
　Parting hath gone by!

Say! how canst thou mourn?
How canst thou rejoice?

Thou art but metal dull!
And yet all our sorrowings,
And all our rejoicings,
   Thou dost feel them all!

God hath wonders many,
Which we cannot fathom,
   Placed within thy form!
When the heart is sinking,
Thou alone canst raise it,
   Trembling in the storm!

THE CASTLE BY THE SEA

BY JOHANN LUDWIG UHLAND

"Hast thou seen that lordly castle,
   That Castle by the Sea?
Golden and red above it
   The clouds float gorgeously.

"And fain it would stoop downward
   To the mirrored wave below;
And fain it would soar upward
   In the evening's crimson glow."

"Well have I seen that castle,
   That Castle by the Sea,
And the moon above it standing,
And the mist rise solemnly."

"The winds and the waves of ocean,
   Had they a merry chime?
Didst thou hear, from those lofty chambers,
The harp and the minstrel's rhyme?"

"The winds and the waves of ocean,
   They rested quietly,

But I heard on the gale a sound of wail,
    And tears came to mine eye."

"And sawest thou on the turrets
    The King and his royal bride?
And the wave of their crimson mantles?
    And the golden crown of pride?

"Led they not forth, in rapture,
    A beauteous maiden there?
Resplendent as the morning sun,
    Beaming with golden hair?"

"Well saw I the ancient parents,
    Without the crown of pride;
They were moving slow, in weeds of woe,
    No maiden was by their side!"

THE BLACK KNIGHT

BY JOHANN LUDWIG UHLAND

'T was Pentecost, the Feast of Gladness,
When woods and fields put off all sadness.
    Thus began the King and spake:
"So from the halls
Of ancient hofburg's walls,
    A luxuriant Spring shall break."

Drums and trumpets echo loudly,
Wave the crimson banners proudly,
    From balcony the King looked on;
In the play of spears,
Fell all the cavaliers,
Before the monarch's stalwart son.

To the barrier of the fight
Rode at last a sable Knight.
"Sir Knight! your name and scutcheon, say!"

"Should I speak it here,
Ye would stand aghast with fear;
    I am a Prince of mighty sway!"

When he rode into the lists,
The arch of heaven grew black with mists,
    And the castle 'gan to rock;
At the first blow,
Fell the youth from saddle-bow,
    Hardly rises from the shock.

Pipe and viol call the dances,
Torch-light through the high halls glances;
    Waves a mighty shadow in;
With manner bland
Doth ask the maiden's hand,
    Doth with her the dance begin.

Danced in sable iron sark,
Danced a measure weird and dark,
    Coldly clasped her limbs around;
From breast and hair
Down fall from her the fair
    Flowerets, faded, to the ground.

To the sumptuous banquet came
Every Knight and every Dame,
'Twixt son and daughter all distraught,
With mournful mind
The ancient King reclined,
Gazed at them in silent thought.

Pale the children both did look,
But the guest a beaker took:
    "Golden wine will make you whole!"
The children drank,
Gave many a courteous thank:
        "O, that draught was very cool!"

Each the father's breast embraces,
Son and daughter; and their faces
   Colorless grow utterly;
Whichever way
Looks the fear-struck father gray,
   He beholds his children die.

"Woe! the blessed children both
Takest thou in the joy of youth;
   Take me, too, the joyless father!"
Spake the grim Guest,
From his hollow, cavernous breast;
   "Roses in the spring I gather!"

SONG OF THE SILENT LAND

BY JOHAN GAUDENZ VON SALISSEEWIS

Into the Silent Land!
Ah! who shall lead us thither?
Clouds in the evening sky more darkly gather,
And shattered wrecks lie thicker on the strand.
Who leads us with a gentle hand
Thither, O thither,
Into the Silent Land?

Into the Silent Land!
To you, ye boundless regions
Of all perfection! Tender morning-visions
Of beauteous souls! The Future's pledge and band!
Who in Life's battle firm doth stand,
Shall bear Hope's tender blossoms
Into the Silent Land!

O Land! O Land!
For all the broken-hearted
The mildest herald by our fate allotted,
Beckons, and with inverted torch doth stand
To lead us with a gentle hand

To the land of the great Departed,
Into the Silent Land!

THE LUCK OF EDENHALL

BY JOHAN LUDWIG UHLAND

OF Edenhall, the youthful Lord
Bids sound the festal trumpet's call;
He rises at the banquet board,
And cries, 'mid the drunken revellers all,
"Now bring me the Luck of Edenhall!"

The butler hears the words with pain,
The house's oldest seneschal,
Takes slow from its silken cloth again
The drinking-glass of crystal tall;
They call it The Luck of Edenhall.

Then said the Lord: "This glass to praise,
Fill with red wine from Portugal!"
The graybeard with trembling hand obeys;
A purple light shines over all,
It beams from the Luck of Edenhall.

Then speaks the Lord, and waves it light:
"This glass of flashing crystal tall
Gave to my sires the Fountain-Sprite;
She wrote in it, If this glass doth fall,
Farewell then, O Luck of Edenhall!

"'T was right a goblet the Fate should be
Of the joyous race of Edenhall!
Deep draughts drink we right willingly:
And willingly ring, with merry call,
Kling! klang! to the Luck of Edenhall!"

First rings it deep, and full, and mild,
Like to the song of a nightingale

Then like the roar of a torrent wild;
Then mutters at last like the thunder's fall,
The glorious Luck of Edenhall.

"For its keeper takes a race of might,
The fragile goblet of crystal tall;
It has lasted longer than is right;
King! klang!—with a harder blow than all
Will I try the Luck of Edenhall!"

As the goblet ringing flies apart,
Suddenly cracks the vaulted hall;
And through the rift, the wild flames start;
The guests in dust are scattered all,
With the breaking Luck of Edenhall!

In storms the foe, with fire and sword;
He in the night had scaled the wall,
Slain by the sword lies the youthful Lord,
But holds in his hand the crystal tall,
The shattered Luck of Edenhall.

On the morrow the butler gropes alone,
The graybeard in the desert hall,
He seeks his Lord's burnt skeleton,
He seeks in the dismal ruin's fall
The shards of the Luck of Edenhall.

"The stone wall," saith he, "doth fall aside,
Down must the stately columns fall;
Glass is this earth's Luck and Pride;
In atoms shall fall this earthly ball
One day like the Luck of Edenhall!"

THE TWO LOCKS OF HAIR

BY GUSTAV PFIZER

A youth, light-hearted and content,
   I wander through the world
Here, Arab-like, is pitched my tent
   And straight again is furled.

Yet oft I dream, that once a wife
   Close in my heart was locked,
And in the sweet repose of life
   A blessed child I rocked.

I wake! Away that dream,—away!
   Too long did it remain!
So long, that both by night and day
   It ever comes again.

The end lies ever in my thought;
   To a grave so cold and deep
The mother beautiful was brought;
   Then dropt the child asleep.

But now the dream is wholly o'er,
   I bathe mine eyes and see;
And wander through the world once more,
   A youth so light and free.

Two locks—and they are wondrous fair—
   Left me that vision mild;
The brown is from the mother's hair,
   The blond is from the child.

And when I see that lock of gold,
   Pale grows the evening-red;
And when the dark lock I behold,
   I wish that I were dead.

THE HEMLOCK TREE.

O hemlock tree! O hemlock tree! how faithful are thy branches!
    Green not alone in summer time,
    But in the winter's frost and rime!
O hemlock tree! O hemlock tree! how faithful are thy branches!

O maiden fair! O maiden fair! how faithless is thy bosom!
    To love me in prosperity,
    And leave me in adversity!
O maiden fair! O maiden fair! how faithless is thy bosom!

The nightingale, the nightingale, thou tak'st for thine example!
    So long as summer laughs she sings,
    But in the autumn spreads her wings.
The nightingale, the nightingale, thou tak'st for thine example!

The meadow brook, the meadow brook, is mirror of thy
  falsehood!
    It flows so long as falls the rain,
    In drought its springs soon dry again.
The meadow brook, the meadow brook, is mirror of thy
  falsehood!

ANNIE OF THARAW

BY SIMON DACH

Annie of Tharaw, my true love of old,
She is my life, and my goods, and my gold.

Annie of Tharaw, her heart once again
To me has surrendered in joy and in pain.

Annie of Tharaw, my riches, my good,
Thou, O my soul, my flesh, and my blood!

Then come the wild weather, come sleet or come snow,
We will stand by each other, however it blow.

Oppression, and sickness, and sorrow, and pain
Shall be to our true love as links to the chain.

As the palm-tree standeth so straight and so tall,
The more the hail beats, and the more the rains fall,—

So love in our hearts shall grow mighty and strong,
Through crosses, through sorrows, through manifold wrong.

Shouldst thou be torn from me to wander alone
In a desolate land where the sun is scarce known,—

Through forests I'll follow, and where the sea flows,
Through ice, and through iron, through armies of foes,

Annie of Tharaw, my light and my sun,
The threads of our two lives are woven in one.

Whate'er I have bidden thee thou hast obeyed,
Whatever forbidden thou hast not gainsaid.

How in the turmoil of life can love stand,
Where there is not one heart, and one mouth, and one hand?

Some seek for dissension, and trouble, and strife;
Like a dog and a cat live such man and wife.

Annie of Tharaw, such is not our love;
Thou art my lambkin, my chick, and my dove.

Whate'er my desire is, in thine may be seen;
I am king of the household, and thou art its queen.

It is this, O my Annie, my heart's sweetest rest,
That makes of us twain but one soul in one breast.

This turns to a heaven the hut where we dwell;
While wrangling soon changes a home to a hell.

THE STATUE OVER THE CATHEDRAL DOOR

BY JULIUS MOSEN

Forms of saints and kings are standing
    The cathedral door above;
Yet I saw but one among them
    Who hath soothed my soul with love.

In his mantle,—wound about him,
    As their robes the sowers wind,—
Bore he swallows and their fledglings,
    Flowers and weeds of every kind.

And so stands he calm and childlike,
    High in wind and tempest wild;
O, were I like him exalted,
    I would be like him, a child!

And my songs,—green leaves and blossoms,—
    To the doors of heaven would hear,
Calling even in storm and tempest,
    Round me still these birds of air.

THE LEGEND OF THE CROSSBILL

BY JULIUS MOSEN

On the cross the dying Saviour
    Heavenward lifts his eyelids calm,
Feels, but scarcely feels, a trembling
    In his pierced and bleeding palm.

And by all the world forsaken,
    Sees he how with zealous care

At the ruthless nail of iron
 A little bird is striving there.

Stained with blood and never tiring,
 With its beak it doth not cease,
From the cross 't would free the Saviour,
 Its Creator's Son release.

And the Saviour speaks in mildness:
 "Blest be thou of all the good!
Bear, as token of this moment,
 Marks of blood and holy rood!"

And that bird is called the crossbill;
 Covered all with blood so clear,
In the groves of pine it singeth
 Songs, like legends, strange to hear.

THE SEA HATH ITS PEARLS

BY HEINRICH HEINE

The sea hath its pearls,
 The heaven hath its stars;
But my heart, my heart,
 My heart hath its love.

Great are the sea and the heaven;
 Yet greater is my heart,
And fairer than pearls and stars
 Flashes and beams my love.

Thou little, youthful maiden,
 Come unto my great heart;
My heart, and the sea, and the heaven
 Are melting away with love!

POETIC APHORISMS

FROM THE SINNGEDICHTE OF FRIEDRICH VON LOGAU

MONEY

Whereunto is money good?
Who has it not wants hardihood,
Who has it has much trouble and care,
Who once has had it has despair.

THE BEST MEDICINES

Joy and Temperance and Repose
Slam the door on the doctor's nose.

SIN

Man-like is it to fall into sin,
Fiend-like is it to dwell therein,
Christ-like is it for sin to grieve,
God-like is it all sin to leave.

POVERTY AND BLINDNESS

A blind man is a poor man, and blind a poor man is;
For the former seeth no man, and the latter no man sees.

LAW OF LIFE

Live I, so live I,
To my Lord heartily,
To my Prince faithfully,
To my Neighbor honestly.
Die I, so die I.

CREEDS

Lutheran, Popish, Calvinistic, all these creeds and doctrines three
Extant are; but still the doubt is, where Christianity may be.

THE RESTLESS HEART

A millstone and the human heart are driven ever round;

If they have nothing else to grind, they must themselves be
ground.

CHRISTIAN LOVE

Whilom Love was like a fire, and warmth and comfort it bespoke;
But, alas! it now is quenched, and only bites us, like the smoke.

ART AND TACT

Intelligence and courtesy not always are combined;
Often in a wooden house a golden room we find.

RETRIBUTION

Though the mills of God grind slowly, yet they grind exceeding
small;
Though with patience he stands waiting, with exactness grinds
he all.

TRUTH

When by night the frogs are croaking, kindle but a torch's fire,
Ha! how soon they all are silent! Thus Truth silences the liar.

RHYMES

If perhaps these rhymes of mine should sound not well in
strangers' ears,
They have only to bethink them that it happens so with theirs;
For so long as words, like mortals, call a fatherland their own,
They will be most highly valued where they are best and
longest known.

SILENT LOVE

Who love would seek,
    Let him love evermore
And seldom speak;
    For in love's domain
    Silence must reign;
Or it brings the heart
    Smart
            And pain.

BLESSED ARE THE DEAD

BY SIMON DACH

Oh, how blest are ye whose toils are ended!
Who, through death, have unto God ascended!
Ye have arisen
From the cares which keep us still in prison.

We are still as in a dungeon living,
Still oppressed with sorrow and misgiving;
Our undertakings
Are but toils, and troubles, and heart-breakings.

Ye meanwhile, are in your chambers sleeping,
Quiet, and set free from all our weeping;
No cross nor trial
Hinders your enjoyments with denial.

Christ has wiped away your tears for ever;
Ye have that for which we still endeavor.
To you are chanted
Songs which yet no mortal ear have haunted.

Ah! who would not, then, depart with gladness,
To inherit heaven for earthly sadness?
Who here would languish
Longer in bewailing and in anguish?

Come, O Christ, and loose the chains that bind us!
Lead us forth, and cast this world behind us!
With Thee, the Anointed,
Finds the soul its joy and rest appointed.

WANDERER'S NIGHT-SONGS

BY JOHANN WOLFGANG VON GOETHE

I

Thou that from the heavens art,
Every pain and sorrow stillest,
And the doubly wretched heart
Doubly with refreshment fillest,
I am weary with contending!
Why this rapture and unrest?
Peace descending
Come, ah, come into my breast!

II

O'er all the hill-tops
Is quiet now,
In all the tree-tops
Hearest thou
Hardly a breath;
The birds are asleep in the trees:
Wait; soon like these
Thou too shalt rest.

REMORSE

BY AUGUST VON PLATEN

How I started up in the night, in the night,
  Drawn on without rest or reprieval!
The streets, with their watchmen, were lost to my sight,
  As I wandered so light
  In the night, in the night,
Through the gate with the arch mediaeval.

The mill-brook rushed from the rocky height,
  I leaned o'er the bridge in my yearning;

Deep under me watched I the waves in their flight,
    As they glided so light
    In the night, in the night,
Yet backward not one was returning.

O'erhead were revolving, so countless and bright,
    The stars in melodious existence;
And with them the moon, more serenely bedight;—
    They sparkled so light
    In the night, in the night,
Through the magical, measureless distance.

And upward I gazed in the night, in the night,
    And again on the waves in their fleeting;
Ah woe! thou hast wasted thy days in delight,
    Now silence thou light,
    In the night, in the night,
The remorse in thy heart that is beating.

FORSAKEN.

Something the heart must have to cherish,
    Must love and joy and sorrow learn,
Something with passion clasp or perish,
    And in itself to ashes burn.

So to this child my heart is clinging,
    And its frank eyes, with look intense,
Me from a world of sin are bringing
    Back to a world of innocence.

Disdain must thou endure forever;
    Strong may thy heart in danger be!
Thou shalt not fail! but ah, be never
    False as thy father was to me.

Never will I forsake thee, faithless,
    And thou thy mother ne'er forsake,

Until her lips are white and breathless,
   Until in death her eyes shall break.

ALLAH

BY SIEGFRIED AUGUST MAHLMANN

Allah gives light in darkness,
   Allah gives rest in pain,
Cheeks that are white with weeping
   Allah paints red again.

The flowers and the blossoms wither,
Years vanish with flying fleet;
But my heart will live on forever,
   That here in sadness beat.

Gladly to Allah's dwelling
   Yonder would I take flight;
There will the darkness vanish,
   There will my eyes have sight.

* * * * *

FROM THE ANGLO-SAXON

THE GRAVE

For thee was a house built
Ere thou wast born,
For thee was a mould meant
Ere thou of mother camest.
But it is not made ready,
Nor its depth measured,

Nor is it seen
How long it shall be.
Now I bring thee
Where thou shalt be;
Now I shall measure thee,
And the mould afterwards.

Thy house is not
Highly timbered,
It is unhigh and low;
When thou art therein,
The heel-ways are low,
The side-ways unhigh.
The roof is built
Thy breast full nigh,
So thou shalt in mould
Dwell full cold,
Dimly and dark.

Doorless is that house,
And dark it is within;
There thou art fast detained
And Death hath the key.
Loathsome is that earth-house,
And grim within to dwell.
There thou shalt dwell,
And worms shall divide thee.
Thus thou art laid,

And leavest thy friends
Thou hast no friend,
Who will come to thee,
Who will ever see
How that house pleaseth thee;
Who will ever open
The door for thee,
And descend after thee;
For soon thou art loathsome
And hateful to see.

Thus then, much care-worn,
The son of Healfden
Sorrowed evermore,
Nor might the prudent hero
His woes avert.
The war was too hard,
Too loath and longsome,
That on the people came,
Dire wrath and grim,
Of night-woes the worst.
This from home heard
Higelac's Thane,
Good among the Goths,
Grendel's deeds.
He was of mankind
In might the strongest,
At that day
Of this life,
Noble and stalwart.
He bade him a sea-ship,
A goodly one, prepare.
Quoth he, the war-king,
Over the swan's road,
Seek he would
The mighty monarch,
Since he wanted men.
For him that journey
His prudent fellows
Straight made ready,
Those that loved him.
They excited their souls,
The omen they beheld.
Had the good-man
Of the Gothic people
Champions chosen,
Of those that keenest
He might find,

Some fifteen men.
The sea-wood sought he.
The warrior showed,
Sea-crafty man!
The land-marks,
And first went forth.
The ship was on the waves,
Boat under the cliffs.
The barons ready
To the prow mounted.
The streams they whirled
The sea against the sands.
The chieftains bore
On the naked breast
Bright ornaments,
War-gear, Goth-like.
The men shoved off,
Men on their willing way,
The bounden wood.
　　Then went over the sea-waves,
Hurried by the wind,
The ship with foamy neck,
Most like a sea-fowl,
Till about one hour
Of the second day
The curved prow
Had passed onward
So that the sailors
The land saw,
The shore-cliffs shining,
Mountains steep,
And broad sea-noses.
Then was the sea-sailing
Of the Earl at an end.
　　Then up speedily
The Weather people
On the land went,
The sea-bark moored,
Their mail-sarks shook,

Their war-weeds.
God thanked they,
That to them the sea-journey
Easy had been.

Then from the wall beheld
The warden of the Scyldings,
He who the sea-cliffs
Had in his keeping,
Bear o'er the balks
The bright shields,
The war-weapons speedily.
Him the doubt disturbed
In his mind's thought,
What these men might be.

Went then to the shore,
On his steed riding,
The Thane of Hrothgar.
Before the host he shook
His warden's-staff in hand,
In measured words demanded:

"What men are ye
War-gear wearing,
Host in harness,
Who thus the brown keel
Over the water-street
Leading come
Hither over the sea?

I these boundaries
As shore-warden hold,
That in the Land of the Danes
Nothing loathsome
With a ship-crew
Scathe us might. . . .
Ne'er saw I mightier
Earl upon earth
Than is your own,
Hero in harness.
Not seldom this warrior
Is in weapons distinguished;

Never his beauty belies him,
His peerless countenance!
Now would I fain
Your origin know,
Ere ye forth
As false spies
Into the Land of the Danes
Farther fare.
Now, ye dwellers afar-off!
Ye sailors of the sea!
Listen to my
One-fold thought.
Quickest is best
To make known
Whence your coming may be."

THE SOUL'S COMPLAINT AGAINST THE BODY

FROM THE ANGLO-SAXON

Much it behoveth
Each one of mortals,
That he his soul's journey
In himself ponder,
How deep it may be.
When Death cometh,
The bonds he breaketh
By which were united
The soul and the body.

Long it is thenceforth
Ere the soul taketh
From God himself
Its woe or its weal;
As in the world erst,
Even in its earth-vessel,
It wrought before.

The soul shall come
Wailing with loud voice,
After a sennight,
The soul, to find
The body
That it erst dwelt in;—
Three hundred winters,
Unless ere that worketh
The Eternal Lord,
The Almighty God,
The end of the world.

Crieth then, so care-worn,
With cold utterance,
And speaketh grimly,
The ghost to the dust:
"Dry dust! thou dreary one!
How little didst thou labor for me!
In the foulness of earth
Thou all wearest away
Like to the loam!
Little didst thou think
How thy soul's journey
Would be thereafter,
When from the body
It should be led forth."

FROM THE FRENCH

SONG

FROM THE PARADISE OF LOVE

Hark! hark!
Pretty lark!
Little heedest thou my pain!
But if to these longing arms
Pitying Love would yield the charms
Of the fair
With smiling air,
Blithe would beat my heart again.

Hark! hark!
Pretty lark!
Little heedest thou my pain!
Love may force me still to bear,
While he lists, consuming care;
But in anguish
Though I languish,
Faithful shall my heart remain.

Hark! hark!
Pretty lark!
Little heedest thou my pain!
Then cease, Love, to torment me so;
But rather than all thoughts forego
Of the fair
With flaxen hair,
Give me back her frowns again.

Hark! hark!
Pretty lark!
Little heedest thou my pain!

SONG

And whither goest thou, gentle sigh,
    Breathed so softly in my ear?
    Say, dost thou bear his fate severe
To Love's poor martyr doomed to die?
Come, tell me quickly,—do not lie;
    What secret message bring'st thou here?
And whither goest thou, gentle sigh,
    Breathed so softly in my ear?
May heaven conduct thee to thy will
    And safely speed thee on thy way;
    This only I would humbly pray,—
Pierce deep,—but oh! forbear to kill.
And whither goest thou, gentle sigh,
    Breathed so softly in my ear?

THE RETURN OF SPRING

BY CHARLES D'ORLEANS

Now Time throws off his cloak again
Of ermined frost, and wind, and rain,
And clothes him in the embroidery
Of glittering sun and clear blue sky.
With beast and bird the forest rings,
Each in his jargon cries or sings;
And Time throws off his cloak again.
Of ermined frost, and wind, and rain.

River, and fount, and tinkling brook
Wear in their dainty livery
Drops of silver jewelry;
In new-made suit they merry look;
And Time throws off his cloak again
Of ermined frost, and wind, and rain.

SPRING

BY CHARLES D'ORLEANS

Gentle Spring! in sunshine clad,
    Well dost thou thy power display!
For Winter maketh the light heart sad,
    And thou, thou makest the sad heart gay.
He sees thee, and calls to his gloomy train,
The sleet, and the snow, and the wind, and the rain;
And they shrink away, and they flee in fear,
    When thy merry step draws near.
Winter giveth the fields and the trees, so old,
    Their beards of icicles and snow;
And the rain, it raineth so fast and cold,
    We must cower over the embers low;
And, snugly housed from the wind and weather,
Mope like birds that are changing feather.
But the storm retires, and the sky grows clear,
    When thy merry step draws near.
Winter maketh the sun in the gloomy sky
    Wrap him round with a mantle of cloud;
But, Heaven be praised, thy step is nigh;
    Thou tearest away the mournful shroud,
And the earth looks bright, and Winter surly,
Who has toiled for naught both late and early,
Is banished afar by the new-born year,
    When thy merry step draws near.

THE CHILD ASLEEP

BY CLOTILDE DE SURVILLE

Sweet babe! true portrait of thy father's face,
    Sleep on the bosom that thy lips have pressed!
Sleep, little one; and closely, gently place
    Thy drowsy eyelid on thy mother's breast.
Upon that tender eye, my little friend,
    Soft sleep shall come, that cometh not to me!

I watch to see thee, nourish thee, defend;
    'T is sweet to watch for thee, alone for thee!
His arms fall down; sleep sits upon his brow;
    His eye is closed; he sleeps, nor dreams of harm.
Wore not his cheek the apple's ruddy glow,
    Would you not say he slept on Death's cold arm?

Awake, my boy! I tremble with affright!
    Awake, and chase this fatal thought! Unclose
Thine eye but for one moment on the light!
    Even at the price of thine, give me repose!
Sweet error! he but slept, I breathe again;
    Come, gentle dreams, the hour of sleep beguile!
O, when shall he, for whom I sigh in vain,
    Beside me watch to see thy waking smile?

DEATH OF ARCHBISHOP TURPIN

FROM THE CHANSON DE ROLAND

The Archbishop, whom God loved in high degree,
Beheld his wounds all bleeding fresh and free;
And then his cheek more ghastly grew and wan,
And a faint shudder through his members ran.
Upon the battle-field his knee was bent;
Brave Roland saw, and to his succor went,
Straightway his helmet from his brow unlaced,
And tore the shining hauberk from his breast.
Then raising in his arms the man of God,
Gently he laid him on the verdant sod.
"Rest, Sire," he cried,—"for rest thy suffering needs."
The priest replied, "Think but of warlike deeds!
The field is ours; well may we boast this strife!
But death steals on,—there is no hope of life;
In paradise, where Almoners live again,
There are our couches spread, there shall we rest from pain."

Sore Roland grieved; nor marvel I, alas!
That thrice he swooned upon the thick green grass.

When he revived, with a loud voice cried he,
"O Heavenly Father! Holy Saint Marie!
Why lingers death to lay me in my grave!
Beloved France! how have the good and brave
Been torn from thee, and left thee weak and poor!"
Then thoughts of Aude, his lady-love, came o'er
His spirit, and he whispered soft and slow,
"My gentle friend!—what parting full of woe!
Never so true a liegeman shalt thou see;—
Whate'er my fate, Christ's benison on thee!
Christ, who did save from realms of woe beneath,
The Hebrew Prophets from the second death."
Then to the Paladins, whom well he knew,
He went, and one by one unaided drew
To Turpin's side, well skilled in ghostly lore;—
No heart had he to smile, but, weeping sore,
He blessed them in God's name, with faith that He
Would soon vouchsafe to them a glad eternity.

The Archbishop, then, on whom God's benison rest,
Exhausted, bowed his head upon his breast;—
His mouth was full of dust and clotted gore,
And many a wound his swollen visage bore.
Slow beats his heart, his panting bosom heaves,
Death comes apace,—no hope of cure relieves.
Towards heaven he raised his dying hands and prayed
That God, who for our sins was mortal made,
Born of the Virgin, scorned and crucified,
In paradise would place him by His side.

Then Turpin died in service of Charlon,
In battle great and eke great orison;—
'Gainst Pagan host alway strong champion;
God grant to him His holy benison.

THE BLIND GIRL OF CASTEL CUILLE

BY JACQUES JASMIN

Only the Lowland tongue of Scotland might
Rehearse this little tragedy aright;
Let me attempt it with an English quill;
And take, O Reader, for the deed the will.

I

At the foot of the mountain height
Where is perched Castel Cuille,
When the apple, the plum, and the almond tree
In the plain below were growing white,
This is the song one might perceive
On a Wednesday morn of Saint Joseph's Eve:

"The roads should blossom, the roads should bloom,
So fair a bride shall leave her home!
Should blossom and bloom with garlands gay,
So fair a bride shall pass to-day!"

This old Te Deum, rustic rites attending,
Seemed from the clouds descending;
When lo! a merry company
Of rosy village girls, clean as the eye,
Each one with her attendant swain,
Came to the cliff, all singing the same strain;
Resembling there, so near unto the sky,
Rejoicing angels, that kind Heaven has sent
For their delight and our encouragement.
Together blending,
And soon descending
The narrow sweep
Of the hillside steep,
They wind aslant
Towards Saint Amant,
Through leafy alleys

Of verdurous valleys
With merry sallies
Singing their chant:

"The roads should blossom, the roads should bloom,
So fair a bride shall leave her home!
Should blossom and bloom with garlands gay,
So fair a bride shall pass to-day!

It is Baptiste, and his affianced maiden,
With garlands for the bridal laden!

The sky was blue; without one cloud of gloom,
    The sun of March was shining brightly,
And to the air the freshening wind gave lightly
    Its breathings of perfume.

When one beholds the dusky hedges blossom,
A rustic bridal, oh! how sweet it is!
    To sounds of joyous melodies,
That touch with tenderness the trembling bosom,
            A band of maidens
            Gayly frolicking,
            A band of youngsters
            Wildly rollicking!
                Kissing,
                Caressing,
    With fingers pressing,
            Till in the veriest
    Madness of mirth, as they dance,
    They retreat and advance,
            Trying whose laugh shall be loudest and merriest;
    While the bride, with roguish eyes,
Sporting with them, now escapes and cries:
            "Those who catch me
                Married verily
                This year shall be!"

And all pursue with eager haste,
And all attain what they pursue,
And   touch her pretty apron fresh and new,
And the linen kirtle round her waist.

Meanwhile, whence comes it that among
These youthful maidens fresh and fair,
So joyous, with such laughing air,
Baptiste stands sighing, with silent tongue?
And yet the bride is fair and young!
Is it Saint Joseph would say to us all,
That love, o'er-hasty, precedeth a fall?
O no! for a maiden frail, I trow,
Never bore so lofty a brow!
What lovers! they give not a single caress!
To see them so careless and cold to-day,
These are grand people, one would say.
What ails Baptiste? what grief doth him oppress?

It is, that half-way up the hill,
In yon cottage, by whose walls
Stand the cart-house and the stalls,
Dwelleth the blind orphan still,
Daughter of a veteran old;
And you must know, one year ago,
That Margaret, the young and tender,
Was the village pride and splendor,
And Baptiste her lover bold.
Love, the deceiver, them ensnared;
For them the altar was prepared;
But alas! the summer's blight,
The dread disease that none can stay,
The pestilence that walks by night,
Took the young bride's sight away.

All at the father's stern command was changed;
Their peace was gone, but not their love estranged.
Wearied at home, erelong the lover fled;
Returned but three short days ago,

The golden chain they round him throw,
He is enticed, and onward led
To marry Angela, and yet
Is thinking ever of Margaret.

Then suddenly a maiden cried,
"Anna, Theresa, Mary, Kate!
Here comes the cripple Jane!" And by a fountain's side
A woman, bent and gray with years,
Under the mulberry-trees appears,
And all towards her run, as fleet
As had they wings upon their feet.

It is that Jane, the cripple Jane,
Is a soothsayer, wary and kind.
She telleth fortunes, and none complain.
She promises one a village swain,
Another a happy wedding-day,
And the bride a lovely boy straightway.
All comes to pass as she avers;
She never deceives, she never errs.

But for this once the village seer
Wears a countenance severe,
And from beneath her eyebrows thin and white
Her two eyes flash like cannons bright
Aimed at the bridegroom in waistcoat blue,
Who, like a statue, stands in view;
Changing color as well he might,
When the beldame wrinkled and gray
Takes the young bride by the hand,
And, with the tip of her reedy wand
Making the sign of the cross, doth say:—
"Thoughtless Angela, beware!
Lest, when thou weddest this false bridegroom,
Thou diggest for thyself a tomb!"
And she was silent; and the maidens fair
Saw from each eye escape a swollen tear;
But on a little streamlet silver-clear,

What are two drops of turbid rain?
Saddened a moment, the bridal train
Resumed the dance and song again;
The bridegroom only was pale with fear;—
And down green alleys
Of verdurous valleys,
With merry sallies,
They sang the refrain:—

"The roads should blossom, the roads should bloom,
So fair a bride shall leave her home!
Should blossom and bloom with garlands gay,
So fair a bride shall pass to-day!"

II

And by suffering worn and weary,
But beautiful as some fair angel yet,
Thus lamented Margaret,
In her cottage lone and dreary;—

"He has arrived! arrived at last!
Yet Jane has named him not these three days past;
Arrived! yet keeps aloof so far!
And knows that of my night he is the star!
Knows that long months I wait alone, benighted,
And count the moments since he went away!
Come! keep the promise of that happier day,
That I may keep the faith to thee I plighted!
What joy have I without thee? what delight?
Grief wastes my life, and makes it misery;
Day for the others ever, but for me
Forever night! forever night!
When he is gone 't is dark! my soul is sad!
I suffer! O my God! come, make me glad.
When he is near, no thoughts of day intrude;
Day has blue heavens, but Baptiste has blue eyes!
Within them shines for me a heaven of love,
A heaven all happiness, like that above,

No more of grief! no more of lassitude!
Earth I forget,—and heaven, and all distresses,
When seated by my side my hand he presses;
      But when alone, remember all!
Where is Baptiste? he hears not when I call!
A branch of ivy, dying on the ground,
      I need some bough to twine around!
In pity come! be to my suffering kind!
True love, they say, in grief doth more abound!
      What then—when one is blind?

      "Who knows? perhaps I am forsaken!
Ah! woe is me! then bear me to my grave!
      O God! what thoughts within me waken!
Away! he will return! I do but rave!
      He will return! I need not fear!
      He swore it by our Saviour dear;
      He could not come at his own will;
      Is weary, or perhaps is ill!
      Perhaps his heart, in this disguise,
      Prepares for me some sweet surprise!
But some one comes! Though blind, my heart can see!
And that deceives me not! 't is he! 't is he!"

      And the door ajar is set,
      And poor, confiding Margaret
Rises, with outstretched arms, but sightless eyes;
'T is only Paul, her brother, who thus cries:—
      "Angela the bride has passed!
      I saw the wedding guests go by;
Tell me, my sister, why were we not asked?
      For all are there but you and I!"

      "Angela married! and not send
      To tell her secret unto me!
      O, speak! who may the bridegroom be?"
      "My sister, 't is Baptiste, thy friend!"

A cry the blind girl gave, but nothing said;
A milky whiteness spreads upon her cheeks;
   An icy hand, as heavy as lead,
   Descending, as her brother speaks,
   Upon her heart, that has ceased to beat,
   Suspends awhile its life and heat.
She stands beside the boy, now sore distressed,
A wax Madonna as a peasant dressed.

   At length, the bridal song again
   Brings her back to her sorrow and pain.

   "Hark! the joyous airs are ringing!
   Sister, dost thou hear them singing?
   How merrily they laugh and jest!
   Would we were bidden with the rest!
   I would don my hose of homespun gray,
   And my doublet of linen striped and gay;
   Perhaps they will come; for they do not wed
   Till to-morrow at seven o'clock, it is said!"

   "I know it!" answered Margaret;
Whom the vision, with aspect black as jet,
   Mastered again; and its hand of ice
Held her heart crushed, as in a vice!
   "Paul, be not sad! 'T is a holiday;
   To-morrow put on thy doublet gay!
   But leave me now for a while alone."
   Away, with a hop and a jump, went Paul,
   And, as he whistled along the hall,
   Entered Jane, the crippled crone.

   "Holy Virgin! what dreadful heat!
   I am faint, and weary, and out of breath!
   But thou art cold,—art chill as death;
   My little friend! what ails thee, sweet?"
"Nothing! I heard them singing home the bride;
   And, as I listened to the song,
   I thought my turn would come erelong,

Thou knowest it is at Whitsuntide.
Thy cards forsooth can never lie,
To me such joy they prophesy,
Thy skill shall be vaunted far and wide
When they behold him at my side.
And poor Baptiste, what sayest thou?
It must seem long to him;—methinks I see him now!"
Jane, shuddering, her hand doth press:
"Thy love I cannot all approve;
We must not trust too much to happiness;—
Go, pray to God, that thou mayst love him less!"
"The more I pray, the more I love!
It is no sin, for God is on my side!"
It was enough; and Jane no more replied.

Now to all hope her heart is barred and cold;
But to deceive the beldame old
She takes a sweet, contented air;
Speak of foul weather or of fair,
At every word the maiden smiles!
Thus the beguiler she beguiles;
So that, departing at the evening's close,
She says, "She may be saved! she nothing knows!"

Poor Jane, the cunning sorceress!
Now that thou wouldst, thou art no prophetess!
This morning, in the fulness of thy heart,
Thou wast so, far beyond thine art!

III

Now rings the bell, nine times reverberating,
And the white daybreak, stealing up the sky,
Sees in two cottages two maidens waiting,
How differently!

Queen of a day, by flatterers caressed,
The one puts on her cross and crown,
Decks with a huge bouquet her breast,

And flaunting, fluttering up and down,
Looks at herself, and cannot rest,
The other, blind, within her little room,
Has neither crown nor flower's perfume;
But in their stead for something gropes apart,
That in a drawer's recess doth lie,
And, 'neath her bodice of bright scarlet dye,
Convulsive clasps it to her heart.

The one, fantastic, light as air,
'Mid kisses ringing,
And joyous singing,
Forgets to say her morning prayer!

The other, with cold drops upon her brow,
Joins her two hands, and kneels upon the floor,
And whispers, as her brother opes the door,
"O God! forgive me now!"

And then the orphan, young and blind,
Conducted by her brother's hand,
Towards the church, through paths unscanned,
With tranquil air, her way doth wind.
Odors of laurel, making her faint and pale,
Round her at times exhale,
And   in the sky as yet no sunny ray,
But brumal vapors gray.

Near that castle, fair to see,
Crowded with sculptures old, in every part,
Marvels of nature and of art,
And proud of its name of high degree,
A little chapel, almost bare
At the base of the rock, is builded there;
All glorious that it lifts aloof,
Above each jealous cottage roof,
Its sacred summit, swept by autumn gales,
And its blackened steeple high in air,
Round which the osprey screams and sails.

"Paul, lay thy noisy rattle by!"
Thus Margaret said. "Where are we? we ascend!"
         "Yes; seest thou not our journey's end?
Hearest not the osprey from the belfry cry?
The hideous bird, that brings ill luck, we know!
Dost thou remember when our father said,
         The night we watched beside his bed,
         'O daughter, I am weak and low;
Take care of Paul; I feel that I am dying!'
And thou, and he, and I, all fell to crying?
Then on the roof the osprey screamed aloud;
And here they brought our father in his shroud.
There is his grave; there stands the cross we set;
Why dost thou clasp me so, dear Margaret?
         Come in! The bride will be here soon:
Thou tremblest! O my God! thou art going to swoon!"

She could no more,—the blind girl, weak and weary!
A voice seemed crying from that grave so dreary,
"What wouldst thou do, my daughter?"—and she started,
         And quick recoiled, aghast, faint-hearted;
But Paul, impatient, urges evermore
         Her steps towards the open door;
And when, beneath her feet, the unhappy maid
Crushes the laurel near the house immortal,
And with her head, as Paul talks on again,
         Touches the crown of filigrane
         Suspended from the low-arched portal,
         No more restrained, no more afraid,
         She walks, as for a feast arrayed,
And in the ancient chapel's sombre night
         They both are lost to sight.

                    At length the bell,
                    With booming sound,
                    Sends forth, resounding round.
Its hymeneal peal o'er rock and down the dell.
         It is broad day, with sunshine and with rain;

And yet the guests delay not long,
For soon arrives the bridal train,
And with it brings the village throng.

In sooth, deceit maketh no mortal gay,
For lo! Baptiste on this triumphant day,
Mute as an idiot, sad as yester-morning,
Thinks only of the beldame's words of warning.

And Angela thinks of her cross, I wis;
To be a bride is all! The pretty lisper
Feels her heart swell to hear all round her whisper,
"How beautiful! how beautiful she is!".

But she must calm that giddy head,
For already the Mass is said;
At the holy table stands the priest;
The wedding ring is blessed; Baptiste receives it;
Ere on the finger of the bride he leaves it,
He must pronounce one word at least!
'T is spoken; and sudden at the grooms-man's side
"'T is he!" a well-known voice has cried.
And while the wedding guests all hold their breath,
Opes the confessional, and the blind girl, see!
"Baptiste," she said, "since thou hast wished my death,
As holy water be my blood for thee!"
And calmly in the air a knife suspended!
Doubtless her guardian angel near attended,
For anguish did its work so well,
That, ere the fatal stroke descended,
Lifeless she fell!

At eve instead of bridal verse,
The De Profundis filled the air;
Decked with flowers a simple hearse
To the churchyard forth they bear;
Village girls in robes of snow
Follow, weeping as they go;

Nowhere was a smile that day,
No, ah no! for each one seemed to say:—

"The road should mourn and be veiled in gloom,
So fair a corpse shall leave its home!
Should mourn and should weep, ah, well-away!
So fair a corpse shall pass to-day!"

A CHRISTMAS CAROL

FROM THE NOEI BOURGUIGNON DE GUI BAROZAI

I hear along our street
Pass the minstrel throngs;
Hark! they play so sweet,
On their hautboys, Christmas songs!
Let us by the fire
Ever higher
Sing them till the night expire!

In December ring
Every day the chimes;
Loud the gleemen sing
In the streets their merry rhymes.
Let us by the fire
Ever higher
Sing them till the night expire.

Shepherds at the grange,
Where the Babe was born,
Sang, with many a change,
Christmas carols until morn.
Let us by the fire
Ever higher
Sing them till the night expire!

These good people sang
Songs devout and sweet;
While the rafters rang,

There they stood with freezing feet.
                    Let us by the fire
                    Ever higher
Sing them till the night expire.

                    Nuns in frigid veils
                    At this holy tide,
                    For want of something else,
Christmas songs at times have tried.
                    Let us by the fire
                    Ever higher
Sing them fill the night expire!

                    Washerwomen old,
                    To the sound they beat,
                    Sing by rivers cold,
With uncovered heads and feet.
                    Let us by the fire
                    Ever higher
Sing them till the night expire.

                    Who by the fireside stands
                    Stamps his feet and sings;
                    But he who blows his hands
Not so gay a carol brings.
                    Let us by the fire
                    Ever higher
Sing them till the night expire!

CONSOLATION

To M. Duperrier, Gentleman of Aix in Provence, on the
Death of his Daughter.

BY FRANCOISE MALHERBE

Will then, Duperrier, thy sorrow be eternal?
                    And shall the sad discourse

Whispered within thy heart, by tenderness paternal,
Only augment its force?

Thy daughter's mournful fate, into the tomb descending
By death's frequented ways,
Has it become to thee a labyrinth never ending,
Where thy lost reason strays?

I know the charms that made her youth a benediction:
Nor should I be content,
As a censorious friend, to solace thine affliction
By her disparagement.

But she was of the world, which fairest things exposes
To fates the most forlorn;
A rose, she too hath lived as long as live the roses,
The space of one brief morn.

* * * * *

Death has his rigorous laws, unparalleled, unfeeling;
All prayers to him are vain;
Cruel, he stops his ears, and, deaf to our appealing,
He leaves us to complain.

The poor man in his hut, with only thatch for cover,
Unto these laws must bend;
The sentinel that guards the barriers of the Louvre
Cannot our kings defend.

To murmur against death, in petulant defiance,
Is never for the best;
To will what God doth will, that is the only science
That gives us any rest.

TO CARDINAL RICHELIEU

BY FRANCOIS DE MALHERBE

Thou mighty Prince of Church and State,
Richelieu! until the hour of death,
Whatever road man chooses, Fate
Still holds him subject to her breath.
Spun of all silks, our days and nights
Have sorrows woven with delights;
And of this intermingled shade
Our various destiny appears,
Even as one sees the course of years
Of summers and of winters made.

Sometimes the soft, deceitful hours
Let us enjoy the halcyon wave;
Sometimes impending peril lowers
Beyond the seaman's skill to save,
The Wisdom, infinitely wise,
That gives to human destinies
Their foreordained necessity,
Has made no law more fixed below,
Than the alternate ebb and flow
Of Fortune and Adversity.

THE ANGEL AND THE CHILD

BY JEAN REBOUL, THE BAKER OF NISMES

An angel with a radiant face,
 Above a cradle bent to look,
Seemed his own image there to trace,
 As in the waters of a brook.

"Dear child! who me resemblest so,"
 It whispered, "come, O come with me!
Happy together let us go,
 The earth unworthy is of thee!

"Here none to perfect bliss attain;
  The soul in pleasure suffering lies;
Joy hath an undertone of pain,
  And even the happiest hours their sighs.

"Fear doth at every portal knock;
  Never a day serene and pure
From the o'ershadowing tempest's shock
  Hath made the morrow's dawn secure.

"What then, shall sorrows and shall fears
  Come to disturb so pure a brow?
And with the bitterness of tears
  These eyes of azure troubled grow?

"Ah no! into the fields of space,
  Away shalt thou escape with me;
And Providence will grant thee grace
  Of all the days that were to be.

"Let no one in thy dwelling cower,
  In sombre vestments draped and veiled;
But let them welcome thy last hour,
  As thy first moments once they hailed.

"Without a cloud be there each brow;
  There let the grave no shadow cast;
When one is pure as thou art now,
  The fairest day is still the last."

And waving wide his wings of white,
  The angel, at these words, had sped
Towards the eternal realms of light!—
  Poor mother! see, thy son is dead!

ON THE TERRACE OF THE AIGALADES

BY JOSEPH MERY

From this high portal, where upsprings
The rose to touch our hands in play,
We at a glance behold three things—
The Sea, the Town, and the Highway.

And the Sea says: My shipwrecks fear;
I drown my best friends in the deep;
And those who braved icy tempests, here
Among my sea-weeds lie asleep!

The Town says: I am filled and fraught
With tumult and with smoke and care;
My days with toil are overwrought,
And in my nights I gasp for air.

The Highway says: My wheel-tracks guide
To the pale climates of the North;
Where my last milestone stands abide
The people to their death gone forth.

Here, in the shade, this life of ours,
Full of delicious air, glides by
Amid a multitude of flowers
As countless as the stars on high;

These red-tiled roofs, this fruitful soil,
Bathed with an azure all divine,
Where springs the tree that gives us oil,
The grape that giveth us the wine;

Beneath these mountains stripped of trees,
Whose tops with flowers are covered o'er,
Where springtime of the Hesperides
Begins, but endeth nevermore;

Under these leafy vaults and walls,
That unto gentle sleep persuade;
This rainbow of the waterfalls,
Of mingled mist and sunshine made;

Upon these shores, where all invites,
We live our languid life apart;
This air is that of life's delights,
The festival of sense and heart;

This limpid space of time prolong,
Forget to-morrow in to-day,
And leave unto the passing throng
The Sea, the Town, and the Highway.

TO MY BROOKLET

BY JEAN FRANCOIS DUCIS

Thou brooklet, all unknown to song,
Hid in the covert of the wood!
Ah, yes, like thee I fear the throng,
Like thee I love the solitude.

O brooklet, let my sorrows past
Lie all forgotten in their graves,
Till in my thoughts remain at last
Only thy peace, thy flowers, thy waves.

The lily by thy margin waits;—
The nightingale, the marguerite;
In shadow here he meditates
His nest, his love, his music sweet.

Near thee the self-collected soul
Knows naught of error or of crime;
Thy waters, murmuring as they roll,
Transform his musings into rhyme.

Ah, when, on bright autumnal eves,
Pursuing still thy course, shall I
Lisp the soft shudder of the leaves,
And hear the lapwing's plaintive cry?

BARREGES

BY LEFRANC DE POMPIGNAN

I leave you, ye cold mountain chains,
Dwelling of warriors stark and frore!
You, may these eyes behold no more,
Rave on the horizon of our plains.

Vanish, ye frightful, gloomy views!
Ye rocks that mount up to the clouds!
Of skies, enwrapped in misty shrouds,
Impracticable avenues!

Ye torrents, that with might and main
Break pathways through the rocky walls,
With your terrific waterfalls
Fatigue no more my weary brain!

Arise, ye landscapes full of charms,
Arise, ye pictures of delight!
Ye brooks, that water in your flight
The flowers and harvests of our farms!

You I perceive, ye meadows green,
Where the Garonne the lowland fills,
Not far from that long chain of hills,
With intermingled vales between.

You wreath of smoke, that mounts so high,
Methinks from my own hearth must come;
With speed, to that beloved home,
Fly, ye too lazy coursers, fly!

And bear me thither, where the soul
In quiet may itself possess,
Where all things soothe the mind's distress,
Where all things teach me and console.

WILL EVER THE DEAR DAYS COME BACK AGAIN?

Will ever the dear days come back again,
    Those days of June, when lilacs were in bloom,
    And bluebirds sang their sonnets in the gloom
    Of leaves that roofed them in from sun or rain?
I know not; but a presence will remain
    Forever and forever in this room,
    Formless, diffused in air, like a perfume,—
    A phantom of the heart, and not the brain.
Delicious days! when every spoken word
    Was like a foot-fall nearer and more near,
    And a mysterious knocking at the gate
Of the heart's secret places, and we heard
    In the sweet tumult of delight and fear
    A voice that whispered, "Open, I cannot wait!"

AT LA CHAUDEAU

BY XAVIER MARMIER

At La Chaudeau,—'t is long since then:
I was young,—my years twice ten;
All things smiled on the happy boy,
Dreams of love and songs of joy,
Azure of heaven and wave below,
            At La Chaudeau.

At La Chaudeau I come back old:
My head is gray, my blood is cold;
Seeking along the meadow ooze,
Seeking beside the river Seymouse,
The days of my spring-time of long ago
            At La Chaudeau.

At La Chaudeau nor heart nor brain
Ever grows old with grief and pain;
A sweet remembrance keeps off age;
A tender friendship doth still assuage
The burden of sorrow that one may know
        At La Chaudeau.

At La Chaudeau, had fate decreed
To limit the wandering life I lead,
Peradventure I still, forsooth,
Should have preserved my fresh green youth,
Under the shadows the hill-tops throw
        At La Chaudeau.

At La Chaudeau, live on, my friends,
Happy to be where God intends;
And sometimes, by the evening fire,
Think of him whose sole desire
Is again to sit in the old chateau
        At La Chaudeau.

A QUIET LIFE.

Let him who will, by force or fraud innate,
   Of courtly grandeurs gain the slippery height;
   I, leaving not the home of my delight,
   Far from the world and noise will meditate.
Then, without pomps or perils of the great,
   I shall behold the day succeed the night;
   Behold the alternate seasons take their flight,
   And in serene repose old age await.
And so, whenever Death shall come to close
   The happy moments that my days compose,
   I, full of years, shall die, obscure, alone!
How wretched is the man, with honors crowned,
   Who, having not the one thing needful found,
   Dies, known to all, but to himself unknown.

THE WINE OF JURANCON

BY CHARLES CORAN

Little sweet wine of Jurancon,
    You are dear to my memory still!
With mine host and his merry song,
Under the rose-tree I drank my fill.

Twenty years after, passing that way,
    Under the trellis I found again
Mine host, still sitting there au frais,
    And singing still the same refrain.

The Jurancon, so fresh and bold,
    Treats me as one it used to know;
Souvenirs of the days of old
    Already from the bottle flow,

With glass in hand our glances met;
    We pledge, we drink. How sour it is
Never Argenteuil piquette
    Was to my palate sour as this!

And yet the vintage was good, in sooth;
    The self-same juice, the self-same cask!
It was you, O gayety of my youth,
    That failed in the autumnal flask!

FRIAR LUBIN

BY CLEMENT MAROT

To gallop off to town post-haste,
    So oft, the times I cannot tell;
To do vile deed, nor feel disgraced,—
    Friar Lubin will do it well.
But a sober life to lead,
    To honor virtue, and pursue it,

That's a pious, Christian deed,—
  Friar Lubin can not do it.

To mingle, with a knowing smile,
  The goods of others with his own,
And leave you without cross or pile,
  Friar Lubin stands alone.
To say 't is yours is all in vain,
  If once he lays his finger to it;
For as to giving back again,
  Friar Lubin cannot do it.

With flattering words and gentle tone,
  To woo and win some guileless maid,
Cunning pander need you none,—
  Friar Lubin knows the trade.
Loud preacheth he sobriety,
  But as for water, doth eschew it;
Your dog may drink it,—but not he;
  Friar Lubin cannot do it.

ENVOY
  When an evil deed 's to do
  Friar Lubin is stout and true;
  Glimmers a ray of goodness through it,
  Friar Lubin cannot do it.

RONDEL

BY JEAN FROISSART

Love, love, what wilt thou with this heart of mine?
  Naught see I fixed or sure in thee!
I do not know thee,—nor what deeds are thine:
Love, love, what wilt thou with this heart of mine?
  Naught see I fixed or sure in thee!

Shall I be mute, or vows with prayers combine?
  Ye who are blessed in loving, tell it me:

Love, love, what wilt thou with this heart of mine?
  Naught see I permanent or sure in thee!

MY SECRET

BY FELIX ARVERS

My soul its secret has, my life too has its mystery,
A love eternal in a moment's space conceived;
Hopeless the evil is, I have not told its history,
And she who was the cause nor knew it nor believed.
Alas! I shall have passed close by her unperceived,
Forever at her side, and yet forever lonely,
I shall unto the end have made life's journey, only
Daring to ask for naught, and having naught received.
For her, though God has made her gentle and endearing,
She will go on her way distraught and without hearing
These murmurings of love that round her steps ascend,
Piously faithful still unto her austere duty,
Will say, when she shall read these lines full of her beauty,
"Who can this woman be?" and will not comprehend.

FROM THE ITALIAN

THE CELESTIAL PILOT

PURGATORIO II. 13-51.

And now, behold! as at the approach of morning,
  Through the gross vapors, Mars grows fiery red
  Down in the west upon the ocean floor
Appeared to me,—may I again behold it!
  A light along the sea, so swiftly coming,

Its motion by no flight of wing is equalled.
And when therefrom I had withdrawn a little
    Mine eyes, that I might question my conductor,
    Again I saw it brighter grown and larger.
Thereafter, on all sides of it, appeared
    I knew not what of white, and underneath,
    Little by little, there came forth another.
My master yet had uttered not a word,
    While the first whiteness into wings unfolded;
    But, when he clearly recognized the pilot,
He cried aloud: "Quick, quick, and bow the knee!
    Behold the Angel of God! fold up thy hands!
    Henceforward shalt thou see such officers!
See, how he scorns all human arguments,
    So that no oar he wants, nor other sail
    Than his own wings, between so distant shores!
See, how he holds them, pointed straight to heaven,
    Fanning the air with the eternal pinions,
    That do not moult themselves like mortal hair!"
And then, as nearer and more near us came
    The Bird of Heaven, more glorious he appeared,
    So that the eye could not sustain his presence,
But down I cast it; and he came to shore
    With a small vessel, gliding swift and light,
    So that the water swallowed naught thereof.
Upon the stern stood the Celestial Pilot!
    Beatitude seemed written in his face!
    And more than a hundred spirits sat within.
"In exitu Israel de Aegypto!"
    Thus sang they all together in one voice,
    With whatso in that Psalm is after written.
Then made he sign of holy rood upon them,
    Whereat all cast themselves upon the shore,
    And he departed swiftly as he came.

THE TERRESTRIAL PARADISE

PURGATORIO XXVIII. 1-33.

Longing already to search in and round
    The heavenly forest, dense and living-green,
    Which tempered to the eyes the newborn day,
Withouten more delay I left the bank,
    Crossing the level country slowly, slowly,
    Over the soil, that everywhere breathed fragrance.
A gently-breathing air, that no mutation
    Had in itself, smote me upon the forehead,
    No heavier blow, than of a pleasant breeze,
Whereat the tremulous branches readily
    Did all of them bow downward towards that side
    Where its first shadow casts the Holy Mountain;
Yet not from their upright direction bent
    So that the little birds upon their tops
    Should cease the practice of their tuneful art;
But with full-throated joy, the hours of prime
    Singing received they in the midst of foliage
    That made monotonous burden to their rhymes,
Even as from branch to branch it gathering swells,
    Through the pine forests on the shore of Chiassi,
    When Aeolus unlooses the Sirocco.
Already my slow steps had led me on
    Into the ancient wood so far, that I
    Could see no more the place where I had entered.
And lo! my further course cut off a river,
    Which, tow'rds the left hand, with its little waves,
    Bent down the grass, that on its margin sprang.
All waters that on earth most limpid are,
    Would seem to have within themselves some mixture,
    Compared with that, which nothing doth conceal,
Although it moves on with a brown, brown current,
    Under the shade perpetual, that never
    Ray of the sun lets in, nor of the moon.

BEATRICE.

Even as the Blessed, at the final summons,
   Shall rise up quickened, each one from his grave,
   Wearing again the garments of the flesh,
So, upon that celestial chariot,
   A hundred rose ad vocem tanti senis,
   Ministers and messengers of life eternal.
They all were saying, "Benedictus qui venis,"
   And scattering flowers above and round about,
   "Manibus o date lilia plenis."
Oft have I seen, at the approach of day,
   The orient sky all stained with roseate hues,
   And the other heaven with light serene adorned,
And   the sun's face uprising, overshadowed,
   So that, by temperate influence of vapors,
   The eye sustained his aspect for long while;
Thus in the bosom of a cloud of flowers,
   Which from those hands angelic were thrown up,
   And down descended inside and without,
With crown of olive o'er a snow-white veil,
   Appeared a lady, under a green mantle,
   Vested in colors of the living flame.

* * * * *

Even as the snow, among the living rafters
   Upon the back of Italy, congeals,
   Blown on and beaten by Sclavonian winds,
And then, dissolving, filters through itself,
   Whene'er the land, that loses shadow, breathes,
   Like as a taper melts before a fire,
Even such I was, without a sigh or tear,
   Before the song of those who chime forever
   After the chiming of the eternal spheres;
But, when I heard in those sweet melodies
   Compassion for me, more than had they said,
   "O wherefore, lady, dost thou thus consume him?"

The ice, that was about my heart congealed,
    To air and water changed, and, in my anguish,
    Through lips and eyes came gushing from my breast.

* * * * *

Confusion and dismay, together mingled,
    Forced such a feeble "Yes!" out of my mouth,
    To understand it one had need of sight.
Even as a cross-bow breaks, when 't is discharged,
        Too tensely drawn the bow-string and the bow,
    And with less force the arrow hits the mark;
So I gave way beneath this heavy burden,
    Gushing forth into bitter tears and sighs,
    And the voice, fainting, flagged upon its passage.

TO ITALY

BY VINCENZO DA FILICAJA

Italy! Italy! thou who'rt doomed to wear
    The fatal gift of beauty, and possess
    The dower funest of infinite wretchedness
    Written upon thy forehead by despair;
Ah! would that thou wert stronger, or less fair.
    That they might fear thee more, or love thee less,
    Who in the splendor of thy loveliness
    Seem wasting, yet to mortal combat dare!
Then from the Alps I should not see descending
    Such torrents of armed men, nor Gallic horde
    Drinking the wave of Po, distained with gore,
Nor should I see thee girded with a sword
    Not thine, and with the stranger's arm contending,
    Victor or vanquished, slave forever more.

SEVEN SONNETS AND A CANZONE

[The following translations are from the poems of Michael Angelo as revised by his nephew Michael Angelo the Younger, and were made before the publication of the original text by Guasti.]

I
THE ARTIST

Nothing the greatest artist can conceive
    That every marble block doth not confine
    Within itself; and only its design
    The hand that follows intellect can achieve.
The ill I flee, the good that I believe,
    In thee, fair lady, lofty and divine,
    Thus hidden lie; and so that death be mine
    Art, of desired success, doth me bereave.
Love is not guilty, then, nor thy fair face,
    Nor fortune, cruelty, nor great disdain,
    Of my disgrace, nor chance, nor destiny,
If in thy heart both death and love find place
    At the same time, and if my humble brain,
    Burning, can nothing draw but death from thee.

II
FIRE

Not without fire can any workman mould
    The iron to his preconceived design,
    Nor can the artist without fire refine
    And purify from all its dross the gold;
Nor can revive the phoenix, we are told,
    Except by fire. Hence if such death be mine
    I hope to rise again with the divine,
    Whom death augments, and time cannot make old.
O sweet, sweet death! O fortunate fire that burns
    Within me still to renovate my days,
    Though I am almost numbered with the dead!
If by its nature unto heaven returns

This element, me, kindled in its blaze,
Will it bear upward when my life is fled.

III
YOUTH AND AGE

Oh give me back the days when loose and free
    To my blind passion were the curb and rein,
    Oh give me back the angelic face again,
    With which all virtue buried seems to be!
Oh give my panting footsteps back to me,
    That are in age so slow and fraught with pain,
    And fire and moisture in the heart and brain,
    If thou wouldst have me burn and weep for thee!
If it be true thou livest alone, Amor,
    On the sweet-bitter tears of human hearts,
    In an old man thou canst not wake desire;
Souls that have almost reached the other shore
    Of a diviner love should feel the darts,
    And be as tinder to a holier fire.

IV
OLD AGE

The course of my long life hath reached at last,
    In fragile bark o'er a tempestuous sea,
    The common harbor, where must rendered be
    Account of all the actions of the past.
The impassioned phantasy, that, vague and vast,
    Made art an idol and a king to me,
    Was an illusion, and but vanity
    Were the desires that lured me and harassed.
The dreams of love, that were so sweet of yore,
    What are they now, when two deaths may be mine,—
    One sure, and one forecasting its alarms?
Painting and sculpture satisfy no more
    The soul now turning to the Love Divine,
    That oped, to embrace us, on the cross its arms.

V
TO VITTORIA COLONNA

Lady, how can it chance—yet this we see
    In long experience—that will longer last
    A living image carved from quarries vast
    Than its own maker, who dies presently?
Cause yieldeth to effect if this so be,
    And even Nature is by Art at surpassed;
    This know I, who to Art have given the past,
    But see that Time is breaking faith with me.
Perhaps on both of us long life can I
    Either in color or in stone bestow,
    By now portraying each in look and mien;
So that a thousand years after we die,
    How fair thou wast, and I how full of woe,
    And wherefore I so loved thee, may be seen.

VI
TO VITTORIA COLONNA

When the prime mover of my many sighs
    Heaven took through death from out her earthly place,
    Nature, that never made so fair a face,
    Remained ashamed, and tears were in all eyes.
O fate, unheeding my impassioned cries!
    O hopes fallacious! O thou spirit of grace,
    Where art thou now? Earth holds in its embrace
    Thy lovely limbs, thy holy thoughts the skies.
Vainly did cruel death attempt to stay
    The rumor of thy virtuous renown,
    That Lethe's waters could not wash away!
A thousand leaves, since he hath stricken thee down,
    Speak of thee, nor to thee could Heaven convey,
    Except through death, a refuge and a crown.

VII
DANTE

What should be said of him cannot be said;
    By too great splendor is his name attended;
    To blame is easier those who him offended,
    Than reach the faintest glory round him shed.
This man descended to the doomed and dead
    For our instruction; then to God ascended;
    Heaven opened wide to him its portals splendid,
    Who from his country's, closed against him, fled.
Ungrateful land! To its own prejudice
    Nurse of his fortunes; and this showeth well,
    That the most perfect most of grief shall see.
Among a thousand proofs let one suffice,
    That as his exile hath no parallel,
    Ne'er walked the earth a greater man than he.

VIII
CANZONE

Ah me! ah me! when thinking of the years,
The vanished years, alas, I do not find
Among them all one day that was my own!
Fallacious hope; desires of the unknown,
Lamenting, loving, burning, and in tears
(For human passions all have stirred my mind),
Have held me, now I feel and know, confined
Both from the true and good still far away.
I perish day by day;
The sunshine fails, the shadows grow more dreary,
And I am near to fail, infirm and weary.

THE NATURE OF LOVE

BY GUIDO GUINIZELLI

To noble heart Love doth for shelter fly,
As seeks the bird the forest's leafy shade;
Love was not felt till noble heart beat high,
Nor before love the noble heart was made.
    Soon as the sun's broad flame
Was formed, so soon the clear light filled the air;
    Yet was not till he came:
So love springs up in noble breasts, and there
    Has its appointed space,
As heat in the bright flames finds its allotted place.
Kindles in noble heart the fire of love,
As hidden virtue in the precious stone:
This virtue comes not from the stars above,
Till round it the ennobling sun has shone;
    But when his powerful blaze
Has drawn forth what was vile, the stars impart
    Strange virtue in their rays;
And thus when Nature doth create the heart
    Noble and pure and high,
Like virtue from the star, love comes from woman's eye.

FROM THE PORTUGUESE

SONG

BY GIL VICENTE

If thou art sleeping, maiden,
    Awake and open thy door,
'T is the break of day, and we must away,
    O'er meadow, and mount, and moor.

Wait not to find thy slippers,
    But come with thy naked feet;
We shall have to pass through the dewy grass,
    And waters wide and fleet.

FROM EASTERN SOURCES

THE FUGITIVE

A TARTAR SONG

I

"He is gone to the desert land
I can see the shining mane
Of his horse on the distant plain,
As he rides with his Kossak band!

"Come back, rebellious one!
Let thy proud heart relent;
Come back to my tall, white tent,
Come back, my only son!

"Thy hand in freedom shall
Cast thy hawks, when morning breaks,
On the swans of the Seven Lakes,
On the lakes of Karajal.

"I will give thee leave to stray
And pasture thy hunting steeds
In the long grass and the reeds
Of the meadows of Karaday.

"I will give thee my coat of mail,
Of softest leather made,
With choicest steel inlaid;
Will not all this prevail?"

II

"This hand no longer shall
Cast my hawks, when morning breaks,
On the swans of the Seven Lakes,
On the lakes of Karajal.

"I will no longer stray
And pasture my hunting steeds
In the long grass and the reeds
Of the meadows of Karaday.

"Though thou give me thy coat of mall,
Of softest leather made,
With choicest steel inlaid,
All this cannot prevail.

"What right hast thou, O Khan,
To me, who am mine own,
Who am slave to God alone,
And not to any man?

"God will appoint the day
When I again shall be
By the blue, shallow sea,
Where the steel-bright sturgeons play.

"God, who doth care for me,
In the barren wilderness,
On unknown hills, no less
Will my companion be.

"When I wander lonely and lost
In the wind; when I watch at night

Like a hungry wolf, and am white
And covered with hoar-frost;

"Yea, wheresoever I be,
In the yellow desert sands,
In mountains or unknown lands,
Allah will care for me!"

III

Then Sobra, the old, old man,—
Three hundred and sixty years
Had he lived in this land of tears,
Bowed down and said, "O Khan!

"If you bid me, I will speak.
There's no sap in dry grass,
No marrow in dry bones! Alas,
The mind of old men is weak!

"I am old, I am very old:
I have seen the primeval man,
I have seen the great Gengis Khan,
Arrayed in his robes of gold.

"What I say to you is the truth;
And I say to you, O Khan,
Pursue not the star-white man,
Pursue not the beautiful youth.

"Him the Almighty made,
And brought him forth of the light,
At the verge and end of the night,
When men on the mountain prayed.

"He was born at the break of day,
When abroad the angels walk;
He hath listened to their talk,
And he knoweth what they say.

"Gifted with Allah's grace,
Like the moon of Ramazan
When it shines in the skies, O Khan,
Is the light of his beautiful face.

"When first on earth he trod,
The first words that he said
Were these, as he stood and prayed,
There is no God but God!

"And he shall be king of men,
For Allah hath heard his prayer,
And the Archangel in the air,
Gabriel, hath said, Amen!"

THE SIEGE OF KAZAN

Black are the moors before Kazan,
    And their stagnant waters smell of blood:
I said in my heart, with horse and man,
    I will swim across this shallow flood.

Under the feet of Argamack,
    Like new moons were the shoes he bare,
Silken trappings hung on his back,
    In a talisman on his neck, a prayer.

My warriors, thought I, are following me;
    But when I looked behind, alas!
Not one of all the band could I see,
    All had sunk in the black morass!

Where are our shallow fords? and where
    The power of Kazan with its fourfold gates?
From the prison windows our maidens fair
    Talk of us still through the iron grates.

We cannot hear them; for horse and man
    Lie buried deep in the dark abyss!

Ah! the black day hath come down on Kazan!
　　Ah! was ever a grief like this?

THE BOY AND THE BROOK

Down from yon distant mountain height
　　The brooklet flows through the village street;
A boy comes forth to wash his hands,
Washing, yes washing, there he stands,
　　In the water cool and sweet.

Brook, from what mountain dost thou come,
　　O my brooklet cool and sweet!
I come from yon mountain high and cold,
Where lieth the new snow on the old,
　　And melts in the summer heat.

Brook, to what river dost thou go?
　　O my brooklet cool and sweet!
I go to the river there below
Where in bunches the violets grow,
　　And sun and shadow meet.

Brook, to what garden dost thou go?
　　O my brooklet cool and sweet!
I go to the garden in the vale
Where all night long the nightingale
　　Her love-song doth repeat.

Brook, to what fountain dost thou go?
　　O my brooklet cool and sweet!
I go to the fountain at whose brink
The maid that loves thee comes to drink,
And whenever she looks therein,
I rise to meet her, and kiss her chin,
　　And my joy is then complete.

TO THE STORK

Welcome, O Stork! that dost wing
    Thy flight from the far-away!
Thou hast brought us the signs of Spring,
    Thou hast made our sad hearts gay.

Descend, O Stork! descend
    Upon our roof to rest;
In our ash-tree, O my friend,
    My darling, make thy nest.

To thee, O Stork, I complain,
    O Stork, to thee I impart
The thousand sorrows, the pain
    And aching of my heart.

When thou away didst go,
    Away from this tree of ours,
The withering winds did blow,
    And dried up all the flowers.

Dark grew the brilliant sky,
    Cloudy and dark and drear;
They were breaking the snow on high,
    And winter was drawing near.

From Varaca's rocky wall,
    From the rock of Varaca unrolled,
the snow came and covered all,
    And the green meadow was cold.

O Stork, our garden with snow
    Was hidden away and lost,
Mid the rose-trees that in it grow
    Were withered by snow and frost.

FROM THE LATIN

VIRGIL'S FIRST ECLOGUE

MELIBOEUS.

Tityrus, thou in the shade of a spreading beech-tree reclining,
Meditatest, with slender pipe, the Muse of the woodlands.
We our country's bounds and pleasant pastures relinquish,
We our country fly; thou, Tityrus, stretched in the shadow,
Teachest the woods to resound with the name of the fair Amaryllis.

TITYRUS.

O Meliboeus, a god for us this leisure created,
For he will be unto me a god forever; his altar
Oftentimes shall imbue a tender lamb from our sheepfolds.
He, my heifers to wander at large, and myself, as thou seest,
On my rustic reed to play what I will, hath permitted.

MELIBOEUS.

Truly I envy not, I marvel rather; on all sides
In all the fields is such trouble. Behold, my goats I am
    driving,
Heartsick, further away; this one scarce, Tityrus, lead I;
For having here yeaned twins just now among the dense
    hazels,
Hope of the flock, ah me! on the naked flint she hath left
    them.
Often this evil to me, if my mind had not been insensate,
Oak-trees stricken by heaven predicted, as now I remember;
Often the sinister crow from the hollow ilex predicted,
Nevertheless, who this god may be, O Tityrus, tell me.

TITYRUS.

O Meliboeus, the city that they call Rome, I imagined,
Foolish I! to be like this of ours, where often we shepherds
Wonted are to drive down of our ewes the delicate offspring.

Thus whelps like unto dogs had I known, and kids to their
    mothers,
Thus to compare great things with small had I been accustomed.
But this among other cities its head as far hath exalted
As the cypresses do among the lissome viburnums.

MELIBOEUS.

    And what so great occasion of seeing Rome hath possessed
        thee?

TITYRUS.

    Liberty, which, though late, looked upon me in my inertness,
    After the time when my beard fell whiter front me in
        shaving,—
    Yet she looked upon me, and came to me after a long while,
    Since Amaryllis possesses and Galatea hath left me.
    For I will even confess that while Galatea possessed me
    Neither care of my flock nor hope of liberty was there.
    Though from my wattled folds there went forth many a
        victim,
    And the unctuous cheese was pressed for the city ungrateful,
    Never did my right hand return home heavy with money.

MELIBOEUS.

    I have wondered why sad thou invokedst the gods, Amaryllis,
    And for whom thou didst suffer the apples to hang on the
        branches!
    Tityrus hence was absent! Thee, Tityrus, even the pine-trees,
    Thee, the very fountains, the very copses were calling.

TITYRUS.

    What could I do? No power had I to escape from my bondage,
    Nor had I power elsewhere to recognize gods so propitious.
    Here I beheld that youth, to whom each year, Meliboeus,
    During twice six days ascends the smoke of our altars.
    Here first gave he response to me soliciting favor:
    "Feed as before your heifers, ye boys, and yoke up your
        bullocks."

MELIBOEUS.

    Fortunate old man! So then thy fields will be left thee,
    And large enough for thee, though naked stone and the marish
    All thy pasture-lands with the dreggy rush may encompass.
    No unaccustomed food thy gravid ewes shall endanger,
    Nor of the neighboring flock the dire contagion inject them.
    Fortunate old man! Here among familiar rivers,
    And these sacred founts, shalt thou take the shadowy coolness.
    On this side, a hedge along the neighboring cross-road,
    Where Hyblaean bees ever feed on the flower of the willow,
    Often with gentle susurrus to fall asleep shall persuade thee.
    Yonder, beneath the high rock, the pruner shall sing to the breezes,
    Nor meanwhile shalt thy heart's delight, the hoarse wood-pigeons,
    Nor the turtle-dove cease to mourn from aerial elm-trees.

TITYRUS.

    Therefore the agile stags shall sooner feed in the ether,
    And the billows leave the fishes bare on the sea-shore.
    Sooner, the border-lands of both overpassed, shall the exiled
    Parthian drink of the Soane, or the German drink of the Tigris,
    Than the face of him shall glide away from my bosom!

MELIBOEUS.

    But we hence shall go, a part to the thirsty Afries,
    Part to Scythia come, and the rapid Cretan Oaxes,
    And to the Britons from all the universe utterly sundered.
    Ah, shall I ever, a long time hence, the bounds of my country
    And the roof of my lowly cottage covered with greensward
    Seeing, with wonder behold,—my kingdoms, a handful of
        wheat-ears!
    Shall an impious soldier possess these lands newly cultured,
    And these fields of corn a barbarian? Lo, whither discord
    Us wretched people hath brought! for whom our fields we
        have planted!
    Graft, Meliboeus, thy pear-trees now, put in order thy vine-
        yards.
    Go, my goats, go hence, my flocks so happy aforetime.
    Never again henceforth outstretched in my verdurous cavern
    Shall I behold you afar from the bushy precipice hanging.

Songs no more shall I sing; not with me, ye goats, as your
    shepherd,
Shall ye browse on the bitter willow or blooming laburnum.

TITYRUS.

Nevertheless, this night together with me canst thou rest thee
Here on the verdant leaves; for us there are mellowing apples,
Chestnuts soft to the touch, and clouted cream in abundance;
And the high roofs now of the villages smoke in the distance,
And from the lofty mountains are falling larger the shadows.

OVID IN EXILE

AT TOMIS, IN BESSARABIA, NEAR THE MOUTHS OF THE DANUBE.

TRISTIA, Book III., Elegy X.

Should any one there in Rome remember Ovid the exile,
    And, without me, my name still in the city survive;

Tell him that under stars which never set in the ocean
    I am existing still, here in a barbarous land.

Fierce Sarmatians encompass me round, and the Bessi and Getae;
    Names how unworthy to be sung by a genius like mine!

Yet when the air is warm, intervening Ister defends us:
    He, as he flows, repels inroads of war with his waves.

But when the dismal winter reveals its hideous aspect,
    When all the earth becomes white with a marble-like frost;

And when Boreas is loosed, and the snow hurled under Arcturus,
    Then these nations, in sooth, shudder and shiver with cold.

Deep lies the snow, and neither the sun nor the rain can dissolve it;
    Boreas hardens it still, makes it forever remain.

Hence, ere the first ha-s melted away, another succeeds it,
And two years it is wont, in many places, to lie.

And so great is the power of the Northwind awakened, it levels
    Lofty towers with the ground, roofs uplifted bears off.

Wrapped in skins, and with trousers sewed, they contend with the
    weather,
    And their faces alone of the whole body are seen.

Often their tresses, when shaken, with pendent icicles tinkle,
    And their whitened beards shine with the gathering frost.

Wines consolidate stand, preserving the form of the vessels;
    No more draughts of wine,—pieces presented they drink.

Why should I tell you how all the rivers are frozen and solid,
    And from out of the lake frangible water is dug?

Ister,—no narrower stream than the river that bears the
    papyrus,—
    Which through its many mouths mingles its waves with the
    deep;

Ister, with hardening winds, congeals its cerulean waters,
    Under a roof of ice, winding its way to the sea.

There where ships have sailed, men go on foot; and the billows,
    Solid made by the frost, hoof-beats of horses indent.

Over unwonted bridges, with water gliding beneath them,
    The Sarmatian steers drag their barbarian carts.

Scarcely shall I be believed; yet when naught is gained by a
    falsehood,
    Absolute credence then should to a witness be given.

I have beheld the vast Black Sea of ice all compacted,
    And a slippery crust pressing its motionless tides.

'T is not enough to have seen, I have trodden this indurate ocean;
    Dry shod passed my foot over its uppermost wave.

If thou hadst had of old such a sea as this is, Leander!
    Then thy death had not been charged as a crime to the Strait.

Nor can the curved dolphins uplift themselves from the water;
    All their struggles to rise merciless winter prevents;

And though Boreas sound with roar of wings in commotion,
    In the blockaded gulf never a wave will there be;

And the ships will stand hemmed in by the frost, as in marble,
    Nor will the oar have power through the stiff waters to cleave.

Fast-bound in the ice have I seen the fishes adhering,
    Yet notwithstanding this some of them still were alive.

Hence, if the savage strength of omnipotent Boreas freezes
    Whether the salt-sea wave, whether the refluent stream,—

Straightway,—the Ister made level by arid blasts of the Northwind,—
    Comes the barbaric foe borne on his swift-footed steed;

Foe, that powerful made by his steed and his far-flying arrows,
    All the neighboring land void of inhabitants makes.

Some take flight, and none being left to defend their possessions,
    Unprotected, their goods pillage and plunder become;

Cattle and creaking carts, the little wealth of the country,
    And what riches beside indigent peasants possess.

Some as captives are driven along, their hands bound behind them,
    Looking backward in vain toward their Lares and lands.

Others, transfixed with barbed arrows, in agony perish,
    For the swift arrow-heads all have in poison been dipped.

What they cannot carry or lead away they demolish,
    And the hostile flames burn up the innocent cots.

Even when there is peace, the fear of war is impending;
    None, with the ploughshare pressed, furrows the soil any more.

Either this region sees, or fears a foe that it sees not,
    And the sluggish land slumbers in utter neglect.

No sweet grape lies hidden here in the shade of its vine-leaves,
    No fermenting must fills and o'erflows the deep vats.

Apples the region denies; nor would Acontius have found here
    Aught upon which to write words for his mistress to read.

Naked and barren plains without leaves or trees we behold
    here,—
    Places, alas! unto which no happy man would repair.

Since then this mighty orb lies open so wide upon all sides,
    Has this region been found only my prison to be?

TRISTIA, Book III., Elegy XII.

Now the zephyrs diminish the cold, and the year being ended,
    Winter Maeotian seems longer than ever before;

And the Ram that bore unsafely the burden of Helle,
    Now makes the hours of the day equal with those of the
    night.

Now the boys and the laughing girls the violet gather,
 Which the fields bring forth, nobody sowing the seed.

Now the meadows are blooming with flowers of various colors,
 And with untaught throats carol the garrulous birds.

Now the swallow, to shun the crime of her merciless mother,
 Under the rafters builds cradles and dear little homes;

And the blade that lay hid, covered up in the furrows of Ceres,
 Now from the tepid ground raises its delicate head.

Where there is ever a vine, the bud shoots forth from the tendrils,
 But from the Getic shore distant afar is the vine!

Where there is ever a tree, on the tree the branches are swelling,
 But from the Getic land distant afar is the tree!

Now it is holiday there in Rome, and to games in due order
 Give place the windy wars of the vociferous bar.

Now they are riding the horses; with light arms now they are playing,
 Now with the ball, and now round rolls the swift-flying hoop:

Now, when the young athlete with flowing oil is anointed,
 He in the Virgin's Fount bathes, over-wearied, his limbs.

Thrives the stage; and applause, with voices at variance, thunders,
 And the Theatres three for the three Forums resound.

Four times happy is he, and times without number is happy,
 Who the city of Rome, uninterdicted, enjoys.

But all I see is the snow in the vernal sunshine dissolving,
 And the waters no more delved from the indurate lake.

Nor is the sea now frozen, nor as before o'er the Ister
 Comes the Sarmatian boor driving his stridulous cart.

Hitherward, nevertheless, some keels already are steering,
    And on this Pontic shore alien vessels will be.

Eagerly shall I run to the sailor, and, having saluted,
    Who he may be, I shall ask; wherefore and whence he hath
    come.

Strange indeed will it be, if he come not from regions adjacent,
    And incautious unless ploughing the neighboring sea.

Rarely a mariner over the deep from Italy passes,
    Rarely he comes to these shores, wholly of harbors devoid.

Whether he knoweth Greek, or whether in Latin he speaketh,
    Surely on this account he the more welcome will be.

Also perchance from the mouth of the Strait and the waters
    Propontic,
    Unto the steady South-wind, some one is spreading his sails.

Whosoever he is, the news he can faithfully tell me,
    Which may become a part and an approach to the truth.

He, I pray, may be able to tell me the triumphs of Caesar,
    Which he has heard of, and vows paid to the Latian Jove;

And that thy sorrowful head, Germania, thou, the rebellious,
    Under the feet, at last, of the Great Captain hast laid.

Whoso shall tell me these things, that not to have seen will afflict
    me,
    Forthwith unto my house welcomed as guest shall he be.

Woe is me! Is the house of Ovid in Scythian lands now?
    And doth punishment now give me its place for a home?

Grant, ye gods, that Caesar make this not my house and my
    homestead,
    But decree it to be only the inn of my pain.

BIBLIOBAZAAR

The essential book market!

Did you know that you can get any of our titles in large print?

Did you know that we have an ever-growing collection of books in many languages?

Order online:
www.bibliobazaar.com

Find all of your favorite classic books!

Stay up to date with the latest government reports!

At BiblioBazaar, we aim to make knowledge more accessible by making thousands of titles available to you- *quickly and affordably.*

Contact us:
BiblioBazaar
PO Box 21206
Charleston, SC 29413

Made in the USA
Lexington, KY
29 December 2010